BUILD WITH ADOBE

BUILD
WITH
ADOBE

□

MARCIA SOUTHWICK

Third Revised Edition

SWALLOW PRESS

OHIO UNIVERSITY PRESS
ATHENS

Third Edition

99 98 97 96   5 4 3 2

Swallow Press/Ohio University Press books
are printed on acid-free paper. ∞

ISBN 0-8040-0634-2
LIBRARY OF CONGRESS CATALOG CARD NUMBER 61-13263

CONTENTS

LIST OF ILLUSTRATIONS

INTRODUCTION

This book happened because I wanted to build an adobe. It is the result of the research I did, put together in book form for the benefit of other would-be builders, because so little material about adobes seems to be available. I do not pretend to be an authority, only a reporter.

ACKNOWLEDGMENTS

A book like this is always the result of the efforts and interest of many people. It would not have been possible without the cheerful cooperation of all those whose homes are pictured and the kindness of the friends who arranged for many of the interviews and pictures. The nicest people live in adobes!

I owe a special debt to my husband, John, who spent long hours in the darkroom and in checking the manuscript. *Build With Adobe* has been a family project.

SO YOU WANT TO BUILD AN ADOBE?

If you are planning to build an adobe house in New York state, forget it! Or in Illinois or Iowa or Washington. The only way you can join the club is to live in an arid or semi-arid region. Unless they contain a somewhat expensive asphalt stabilizer, adobe bricks will wash away in a hard, direct rain; and they melt like an ice cube in a summer julep if they stand in a puddle.

Further, people in New York would probably roll their eyes and tap their foreheads if you proposed building a mud house there. Out here in the Southwest we are used to them. People have been building mud houses here for several hundred years. And they grow on you. A lot of us think that there is nothing prettier than a little sun-drenched, earth-colored cube of a house or a rambling one story charmer with a private patio behind a high mud wall.

We like them because they are part of our local heritage and because they capture for us the essence of the past. We like them because they are warm in winter and cool in summer. (Those thick walls are a heat reservoir and keep us from feeling any sudden changes in temperature.) They are vermin proof and sound deadening and fire resistant. And they can be cheap to build, especially if you are a do-it-yourselfer.

Even if someone else does all the work, it is possible to have an exciting and highly individual, custom-built house of adobe for the price of a tract house of comparable size. This book is designed to show you ways in which it may be done.

Before you begin to build your house, you should take a look at the way the early New Mexicans built. They worked out solutions to the problems of using a material which is vulnerable to moisture and low in compressive and shearing strength.

They chose well-drained sites with the slope away from the house. They usually laid foundations of stone which prevented moisture from entering the walls by capillary action. By laying the long pine poles or *vigas* which supported their roofs with the tapered ends all one way, they gave the roof a slight pitch which helped the rain water to drain off. *Canales* carried the water from the roof so that it ran away from the house. Flat stones protected the roof parapet from the force of the rain. Sometimes brush "eyebrows" on the extended *vigas* were used to protect the walls from water and sun, and a thick coat of mud plaster also helped to prevent erosion.

Because adobe is structurally weak, they made the walls thick. They kept the wall heights low and the wall spans short unless they were buttressed. Door and window openings were placed away from the corners.

When the Americans came, they added some solutions of their own. They covered the vulnerable adobe with lime plaster and added a brick coping around the roofs and the flat-roofed portals that shaded and protected the walls. And, incidentally, by adding a classic architrave above pairs of windows, furnished with shutters and flanking a formal doorway, they created a facade so pleasing that it is still widely used; and so distinctive that it is designated the Territorial style.

Present-day adobe houses represent a blending of cultures, Indian, Spanish, and American. The Indians were building with adobe when the first Spanish colonists straggled into the Rio Grande valley. The house with the stepped-back upper story, which is often seen in Santa Fe and in Taos, traces its origin to the terraced structures of the Indians. They consisted of tiers of windowless rooms, entered by a ladder through the roof. Ceilings were made of peeled poles set side by side, often in a herringbone pattern and occasionally decorated with color. The walls were often very thick and supported by heavy timbers. They were constructed of rocks set with mud mortar or sometimes entirely of mud which was apparently built up by the handful. The Indians did not know how to use bricks of mud until the Spanish taught them.

The Spanish had been building with mud for centuries, having learned about it from the Moors. Their first homes in New Mexico were clustered together around a central plaza for protection. A few isolated ranch houses which were strongholds as well as shelters were built much like those in Spain with rooms opening into an inner court and outside walls innocent of openings except for a heavy gate giving access to the patio. Walls were often two feet thick. Even after the need for protection ceased, the fort-like appearance was in part retained. The scarcity of glass even in later years dictated small windows. In early colonial days the openings might be filled with a small sheet of mica, covered with animal skins, or protected by a crude grill of peeled poles or wooden shutters. The doors were sometimes only five feet high and two feet wide, thick and paneled or constructed of thick adzed planks of pine or cottonwood and set into doorways with sills a foot high. The houses grew, rambling over the contours of the site, as each son of the family married and added a room for his bride at one end of the paternal home. Wood was sparingly used. Glass and metal were almost nonexistent. The Spanish colonist lived in a backwater of provincial isolation, building with the simplest of tools and making do with what was at hand.

In the mountains, where wood was more plentiful, the early builders turned the rain and snow with pitched roofs of split logs and often built thick walls of pine logs set into the ground side by side and plastered liberally with adobe. Interesting examples of this *jacal* construction are still to be found.

When the Americans came, they too used adobe, but the wedding of adobe and Yankee forms of architecture produced a hybrid strange to Spanish eyes. The Americans used sawn beams and boards on their ceilings and millwork for the trim. Flat boards, nailed together to form a square, formed the posts for the portals and porches. Tops of windows and doors were all on a line. The window panes were small, to be sure, but there were many of them, often placed nine over six or twelve over eight. Window frames were set to the outside of the wall. And inside the house a brick fireplace, built in the middle of the wall, replaced the adobe corner fireplace which had been almost universal.

Some of this Territorial style the Spanish people liked and adopted. The classic architrave over the windows was translated into a simple triangular board which appeared over windows and doors everywhere. With better tools now available to them, they created exuberantly handsome hand-carved doors with elaborate raised panels and copied the formal doorway, often placing rows of tiny panes on each side of the door. In general the Territorial forms became simplified in Spanish hands. In rural villages, where innovations seemed too costly, the old styles remained largely unchanged except for the use of the sawn lumber, more and larger windows, and an interesting folk art adaptation of the carved doors so in vogue. The houses now began to string out along the roads, and single family homes were built instead of the patriarchal complexes of colonial times.

The days of the Territory saw more and varied forms: the pitched roof ranch house, the two story houses with two story porches, dormer windows, gabled roofs, french doors. Then, as other building materials became available, adobe fell out of favor with those who could afford something different.

Today people in New Mexico can build houses of brick, block, wood, and even glass if they should wish it. They build Cape Cod houses and Southern Colonial houses and Spanish Mission houses with red tile roofs. They even make the full circle and build the modern *atrium* house, built around an inner courtyard with a plain facade to the street like the early Spanish houses.

The end of New Mexico's isolation may come in time to mean the end of a regional character. It is not within the scope of this book to consider whether this is good or bad. However, in recent years a determined effort has been made in Santa Fe and elsewhere to preserve a regional flavor by encouraging the revival of interest in adobe architecture. Some extremely interesting houses have resulted. What form will ultimately be known as the Revival style, who can tell?

What sort of adobe will yours be? If your choice is way-out modern or a Castle-in-Spain type which is completely and uniquely "you," I applaud it, for I believe that one's house will function only if it is an expression of one's personal taste, needs, and dreams. If you find the traditional pleasing, by all means build this way; but keep in mind that you are building a house for twentieth-century living rather than creating a museum piece. The old doors and beams that are often collected for adobe houses enhance them from a decorative standpoint and may increase your enjoyment of the house, but the absence of a twentieth-century heating system is excusable only if you cannot afford anything else. Make your own contributions and solutions within the traditional framework. The use of the regional material and the styles which evolved in answer to its limitations makes sense architecturally, but only in so much as they are relevant to the needs of the present day.

WHAT CAN YOU SPEND?

Up to this point your dream house exists as a nebulous vision in your mind's eye. To translate this dream into reality you will need 1.) to decide what you can afford, 2.) to select a site, 3.) to draw up a house plan either by yourself or with an architect, 4.) to select a contractor or decide to do it yourself, 5.) to get an estimate of the cost, 6.) to adjust your plans if necessary to make this estimate conform with your budget, 7.) to arrange for financing, 8.) to construct the house, 9.) to landscape the site and furnish the interior.

Do not minimize the importance of this last step. To skimp on landscaping and decorating or to fail to consider them during the planning stage will do much to detract from the appearance of your new house and from your pleasure in living in it. To build a good house you must think of it as an organic whole with its gardens and furnishings.

It is important, too, to select a site before the actual planning of your home begins. It is easier to draw a plan with the limitations of your site in mind than to hunt for a site which will fit all the requirements of your plan as to size, shape, and orientation.

Naturally the first order of business will be a long, hard look at the budget. Be realistic about this. If you apply for a loan to complete your house, you can be sure that the lender will be. Your income, credit, equities, savings, and obligations will be carefully considered. If you receive a loan, you can be quite confident that you will be able to handle the repayment of that amount.

What sort of yardstick can you use to determine in advance the size of the commitment that you can safely assume? One fourth of your monthly income is often considered the maximum monthly payment that should be made for housing. This figure should include

Eroded walls of abandoned house in Manzano Mountains showing *jacal* construction.

Ruined *portal* of an old adobe still standing in Bernalillo. Wings of varying ages surround a central patio, accessible through a *zaguan*. Note the varying heights of doors and windows. Double doors are hung by a primitive hinge. One side of each door extends beyond the top and bottom stiles. It is rounded to fit into holes in the lintel and threshold, allowing the door to swing. See next picture for detail.

Close-up showing how side of door projects beyond the top rail and fits into a socket in the lintel.

Doorway at Paul Krogdahl residence, Sandoval, while new, illustrates the small doorway with a high sill which was common in early adobes.

Handsome old territorial doorway removed from a ruin in Peralta, NM and installed in a renovated adobe near Espanola, NM.

Zaguan of old adobe in Bernalillo has elaborate dentil molding. Triangular board above window is typical simplification of territorial trim. Note the arrangement of the window panes, twelve over eight.

"Fancy" door in Taos area adobe is survival of handsomely-decorated doors of the territorial period.

Dentil molding enhances simple window trim of the restored adobe of Colonel and Mrs. Judson Miller, Albuquerque.

Brick coping and territorial window trim of the Juan Jose Prada House, Santa Fe. House is said to have been built by Italian artisans brought to Santa Fe by Archbishop Lamy.

not only the mortgage payment but also payment for utilities and insurance and monthly installments for the appliances which become part of the house, such as the washer and dryer. Add to this a figure for the maintenance of the property (about one per cent of the total cost of the house).

The amount of monthly payments to be made on the mortgage will include interest and, in some cases, insurance. The total amount of the charges you pay for using the money you have borrowed will increase with the length of time you take to repay it. For example, each one thousand dollars which you borrow at six per cent interest for ten years will cost you $322.20 in interest charges. Each one thousand dollars which you borrow at six per cent interest for twenty years will cost you $720.80 in interest. Keep in mind that your investment for a house will include not only the original cost but interest charges on your mortgage as well. By extending the loan out over a long period, you may actually pay out more in interest than the original purchase price. You would pay for your house twice over.

To keep the cost of your house down, plan to repay the loan over as short a period as is practical and make a reasonable down payment. Ordinarily it takes less actual cash to buy a house already built than to build one. Remember that you cannot spend your last dollar on the house itself. Decorating, landscaping, and other expenses, such as the cost of moving, may run to as much as twenty-five per cent of the cost of the house. If you plan to build in a rural area, investigate the loan possibilities carefully. Interest rates will be higher in a number of instances, and you may find it difficult or even impossible to arrange for a construction loan.

If you are young and on the way up, you may be able to consider buying a house requiring a larger payment than one quarter of your monthly income, for you may reasonably expect this income to increase within a few years. You must consider also that an expanding family and a larger income may soon create a demand for a larger house than you may need now.

But suppose that your expenses for such items as education or medical care promise to be above average, or suppose that you are nearing retirement and a subsequent curtailment of income. You may not then be able to spend as much. Think through your own personal financial situation before you decide what you can afford to spend.

Some attractive adobes have been built by do-it-yourselfers with a pay-as-you-go budget. I know of one handsome adobe that took several years to complete. The labor was done by the owner and his extended family and friends. Adobes were made on the site. Much of the other building material including huge timbers, seasoned lumber, and windows and doors came from demolished buildings. Time and skill rather than money were invested in hand carved lintels, flooring laid in intricate patterns and sculptured plaster. In the end, the owner had his dream house on a bare bones budget.

Owner-built starter houses which are planned for later expansion allow construction costs to be spread out over a period of years. Hiring a contractor to build a shell and doing all the finish work is another method by which the would-be home owner can stretch a slender budget.

Once you have decided upon a budget and accepted its limitations, which will be chiefly the number of square feet you can expect to build and the type of site you can afford, an almost endless number of possibilities remain open to you. Operating within that budget, you should be able to build a satisfactory and satisfying house. The secret lies in PLANNING!

WHERE WILL YOU PUT IT?

The planning process begins with the selection of a site. As I said, your budget may impose a limit upon the type of site which you can afford. Planning may enable you to buy a bargain priced, odd-shaped lot in a desirable neighborhood and to design a house to fit it which will turn its supposed liabilities into an asset. On the other hand, a little planning ahead may keep you from buying a so-called bargain only to find that the side yard and set-back restrictions will so limit the amount of space upon which you can build that its purchase is impractical. Let us take a look at some of the planning which must go into the selection of a site.

Although it is possible to happen upon a spot with such instant appeal that you must have it in spite of its obvious drawbacks, and thereupon live happily ever after, such a happy ending will rarely occur if you make a purchase from whim or caprice. A house represents a major financial investment. Although the lot or acreage upon which it is placed may be only a fraction of the total cost, an unwise choice can mean the difference between a good investment and a poor one. The pleasure which you get from living in your new home, the amount the property will depreciate, the ease with which you could sell it if the need arose, all depend in some measure upon the choice of a good site.

There is no magic formula for deciding how much to spend for a lot. It may be difficult to get a loan for a cheap house on an expensive lot. An expensive house in a neighborhood of cheaper houses may be a white elephant. One way to keep the cost of the site compatible with the cost of your house is to buy in an area of comparatively new homes in the price range of the one which you propose to build. A factor which may limit what you can spend for your location is the fact that the land on which you build must be owned outright before you can get a construction loan. Include this expenditure in the amount you have earmarked for a down payment in your budget. If you follow the suggestion to have at least twenty per cent of the total investment in your house, you will probably spend almost all of it for your site, and this is not an unreasonable amount to invest.

If you are thinking of building in the country, do not forget that the cheaper cost of land in rural areas is often balanced by the expense you may have in development: drilling a well, putting in a cesspool or septic tank for the disposal of sewage, buying tanks for butane or propane gas, running in electric lines, building an access road, or road maintenance. Rural living may mean a big bill for transportation if some member of the family is regularly employed in town. Fire insurance premiums will jump where there is no municipal water system. Interest rates on mortgages are often higher. Building costs may include extra delivery charges for materials.

On the other hand, if you plan to do much of the construction yourself, building codes in rural areas may be more lenient. It is true that property taxes are lower. Just be sure if you choose a site on the outskirts of a community to escape higher urban taxes and assessments and perhaps to have chickens or horses that your property does not lie in an area marked for future annexation which may one day increase the first and prohibit the latter.

Think ahead wherever you plan to buy to possible changes in the character of the neighborhood. Consider the possibility of future paving and other assessments. Zoning regulations and deed restrictions such as those which set a minimum amount of floor space which can be built or those which limit the styles of architecture to certain types generally act to keep property values higher for a longer period of time. They tend to remain higher in neighborhoods of one family houses where the homes appear to be well kept up and most of the property is owner occupied. Avoid buying along the logical extension of main traffic arteries. What seems today to be a quiet residential street may one day teem with traffic. You cannot hope that your purchase will retain its value indefinitely, but the decline in values can be controlled by buying wisely.

While building codes, zoning, and deed restrictions tend to protect your investment, be sure that you investigate them thoroughly. If you plan to do your own building you must know the minimum re-

quirements for heating and wiring and plumbing that will be acceptable under the local codes and how much of the work you will be
allowed to do yourself. Be sure that any deed restrictions do not prohibit building the size house you plan to erect, and that the construction of an adobe house will not be ruled out by a clause limiting the
architectural character of the section to some particular material or
style. Even if it were not restricted, you would be foolish to put a low
country adobe, for example, in a neighborhood where the houses
were all completely different from it in style, such as Georgian or a
modern split level. The house you propose to build must be somewhat
in keeping architecturally with others in the area. If it is not, you may
experience some difficulty in getting a construction loan or in selling
the property should the need arise.

Keeping all these requirements in mind will help you to spend
wisely the money you have allotted for your site. In addition, you may
be able to stretch your allotment by a trick or two. I have already men-
tioned finding a bargain in an odd-shaped lot. If it is large enough it
may be possible to divide it into two smaller lots, one of which will be
a conventional shape which you can sell, while you keep the less sale-
able odd-shaped piece and design your house to fit it. Or buy a deep,
narrow tract of country land and sell the front half along the road,
keeping the rear portion with an easement for a road into it for yourself. It may be wise to avoid a corner lot. Paving will be higher, and it
is often expensive to protect yourself from the noise and lack of privacy due to traffic on the streets around you. Yet corner lots often sell
for a premium. You might look for a lot with a slope. The level lot is
the cheapest to build on and hence in demand. A sloping site may be
cheaper in price and a real bargain for you if you are able to design a
house to take advantage of it. Adobe houses are obliging about chang-
ing levels to fit the contours of the site, and good drainage is a real
"plus" for adobes! A steeply sloping lot, however, may necessitate the
expense of grading or of excavating into the side of the hill before a
house can be built.

If you are planning to have a contractor build your home, check
into the possibility of buying a lot from a contractor. There may be
several advantages to this. First, a contractor specializing in adobe
construction may be able to offer you a selection of lots in an area
where adobe houses are already being constructed. Since these houses

will be of a like character and age, property values will remain fairly constant in this vicinity for some time. Second, a construction loan will be relatively easy to secure. Third, the price of the lot will be included in the figure for the cost of the house. This may mean that less of your cash reserves are committed at the beginning. Sometimes you will be required to purchase the lot in advance of construction, but this purchase may be all the down payment which he will require. At other times the cost of the lot and the completed house will be lumped into one package, and a modest cash down payment will be all that is needed until construction is completed.

Even if you plan to do much of the work yourself, you may be able to complete an agreement with a contractor allowing you to do that part of the construction which you can handle: painting, laying tile, or installing a brick floor. You will not only be saving a sizeable portion of the cost of the house, but the money you "earn" by doing your own work is all tax free!

Bargains can stretch your building dollar, but many so-called bargains will only result in an expensive education. So beware! If you are offered a lot or acreage at a price much below the going figure for land in the area, investigate carefully. Objectionable noises or odors, excessive winds, a rocky soil, or lots of fill which will skyrocket your building costs could all make your bargain a bad buy at any price. Go slowly and ask questions. Don't be so blinded by a modest price tag that you sacrifice features that will make life easy and pleasant for you, such as proximity to shopping, to work, to recreational facilities, good schools, convenient medical care. Take time to be sure before signing that binder.

If you have been aided in your search by a real estate broker, he will handle the details of the purchase for you, drawing up the binder or payment of earnest money, which is the first step in concluding a deal. As the term "binder" implies, this represents a binding contract between you and the seller. Once it has been accepted and signed by both parties, you cannot withdraw without forfeiting the deposit or earnest money which is required of you, and the seller can be compelled to carry through the terms of the agreement. The amount of earnest money which is required will vary. For his own protection the seller should insist upon an amount large enough that you will not consider forfeiture.

The binder agreement describes the property and gives the purchase price and the manner in which it is to be paid. Like any contract, the binder will be legally valid only if it is concluded between parties legally competent (sane and of legal age) who are agreed as to what the contract involves. The property in question must be legally the seller's to convey, and there must be no intent on the part of either party to defraud the other. Something of value, either money or something less tangible such as a promise to do work, should be exchanged.

Normally the binder agreement is followed by a formal contract of sale in which the legal description of the property is given and the terms and conditions of the sale are fully listed. It must be drawn with great care so that your future rights in and enjoyment of the property are safeguarded. All encumberances and restrictions should be listed. Provision should be made for the apportionment of taxes on the property. It should list the closing costs to be borne by the buyer and the seller and should state if a survey is to be made. It should require the seller to furnish an abstract of title, the condensed history of the title to land, which has been brought up to date, or title insurance for the full value of the property. A title policy insures you against loss resulting from a defective title. Even an examination of the abstract of title, which you should have your attorney perform, will not always bring to light everything that will affect the title to your property. Title insurance, where it can be secured, is a wise thing. For your protection the contract should be made conditional upon the delivery of a good, marketable and/or insurable title. Finally, a date should be set for the delivery of the deed and payment of the purchase price.

A real estate broker can close the sale, either directly or through an escrow agent, perhaps the bank where you arrange a loan or the abstract company which has conducted the title search and prepared an abstract of title. You may also have an attorney or escrow agent handle the closing of title if a broker has not been involved in the sale. In either case, you should receive a closing statement listing the sales price, earnest money, and other down payments, all items charged to you, and the final closing figure. Once this money has been paid, the deed will be delivered to you. The final step in the transaction is the recording of the deed in the county clerk's office by which the transfer of the property to you is made a matter of public record.

HOW DO YOU PLAN
TO GET YOUR MONEY'S WORTH?

The land is now yours, but a further step remains to be taken if you are to get full value from your purchase. You must plan how to place your house upon this site to take full advantage of it.

Even if it is a perfectly flat, fifty-foot city lot, planning may give you more privacy from your neighbors, more use of the available space for outdoor living, sun and wind control, and a more spacious appearance.

It is at this point that the architect usually enters the picture if you plan to consult one, although ideally he should be consulted during your search for the site. From the description of the lot, he designs the size and shape of the proposed dwelling and roughs out the arrangement of rooms. He submits rough drawings showing how the house will be placed on the land to comply with any set-back and side yard restrictions and to meet your special needs. These drawings show you the dimensions of the rooms and the placement of the doors and windows and include a sketch showing how the front of the house will look.

If the rough drawings meet with your approval, the working drawings, drawn to scale and showing in minute detail just how the house is to be constructed, will be prepared. The contractor who builds your house will follow these plans exactly. The architect also draws up a list of specifications in which all the materials and appliances to be used in the house are carefully described. From these specifications and drawings a contractor can make an accurate estimate of what the house will cost. If you should desire it, the architect will also contact contractors for bids and oversee the actual construction.

The completed house should be attractive, well built, and suited both to the site and to your requirements. Through his professional know-how the architect may be able to give you more house for less money than you had dared to hope. A well designed house is more marketable, depreciates less, and pays a daily bonus of pleasure and comfort.

If you are not familiar with the work of local architects, it may be wise to have preliminary interviews with several before you select one. Study houses they have designed, especially the work of those who have become identified with adobe construction. I have a friend whose delightful adobe was designed by an "arty contractor," as she put it.

Contractors often give design services, and if there is a meeting of minds with the prospective homeowner, an entirely satisfactory house which makes good use of its site may result.

It is also entirely possible to design your own adobe with good results. Nor is the process as mysterious as it may look to the novice. Let us consider how you might go about planning a house to make the best use of your land.

The first task is to determine the amount of usable space which lies within its boundaries. In the country this may be restricted by the lay of the land. In the city there will be easements and lot lines and set-back restrictions. While these restrictions are intended to protect the landowner from encroachment by his neighbors, they also rule out many original and creative solutions to the problems of site utilization. This is particularly true of the adobe house which might present a closed facade directly upon a city sidewalk and develop the space to the sides and rear of the property for secluded outdoor living as many of the early adobes were designed.

In addition to the easements and restrictions, your plan may be further affected by local regulations concerning the height of the walls and fences which may be built along the property lines. You can get information about these regulations from the city building department.

Draw the outlines of your plot on paper, using one quarter of an inch for every foot of measurement. Indicate by dotted lines how far from the front and side boundaries you must place the house according to the restrictions. If there are trees on the property, measure

their location from the lot lines and locate them on the sketch. It may
be necessary to have a survey made of a hilly or steeply sloping lot.

The surveyor will indicate the changes in elevation (height) by
contour lines. All the land along each line is at the same elevation.
The distance between lines will represent a certain number of feet
that the elevation changes. For example, each line may indicate a
change of one foot in height. Where it is steep the lines will look
close together. Where the slope is gentle, they will be far apart. Do
not bother with contour lines in your plot plan if there is only a modest variance in grade. Unless you are unusually skillful, leave the design of a house for a steeply sloping site to a competent architect.

When you have finished your drawing, you will have an area
where your house can be located pretty clearly defined, but you will
still have some leeway as to whether it is placed to the front or rear of
the property and to the right or left. Although this may be only a few
feet in any direction it is still worth considering.

If you study the accompanying sketch (p. 151) of a plot plan you
will see that by adding only two and a half feet to the side lot restriction on the south side and three and a half feet to the north side lot
restriction, a driveway and a much used outdoor living area could be
placed at the sides of the house in space all too often useless and hard
to landscape. All the space from lot line to lot line was put to use.
Note that because this limited the width of the house, it has been
placed on the site so that its greatest dimension extends out into the
length of the lot. However, there is ample space to the rear for a turning area and driveway serving both a garage and a double carport
placed at right angles to each other to conserve space. Even the
twenty-five foot set back in front of the house has been utilized to provide off-the-street parking for three automobiles.

By planning to use every foot, the designer met the special needs
of this family which included undercover parking for their travel
trailer to meet the requirements of a stringent city code, but the solution did not result in a house that was freakish or so much a specialty
that it would have little appeal to prospective buyers if it should ever
become necessary to sell it.

In some instances you might wish to place your house as close to
the front of your property as possible in order to take advantage of
space to the rear for secluded outdoor living. In other instances more

comfort, convenience, and privacy might be secured by locating the patio toward the front of the lot behind a screening wall and placing the house close to the rear. If the site is level at the rear but slopes at the front, it may be more economical to build on the level area and create a garden on the slope.

The way you place your house can affect the appearance it presents. Small houses look larger if they are stretched long way across the lot. A larger house might well be placed on a smallish lot with its narrow dimension to the street to keep it from looking hemmed in by its neighbors and to suggest spaciousness by emphasizing the depth of the site.

You must consider not only the best utilization of space when you locate your house but consider also the orientation to the sun and to the prevailing winds. In many New Mexico towns, lots with a western exposure seem to be preferred by buyers because an outdoor living area located at the rear of a house on such a lot would be protected from the hot rays of the late afternoon sun in summer. Whether they realize it or not, they have used a device to control one aspect of the micro-climate of their site. Too often little else is done; yet a great deal can be done when you plan your house to modify the climate about it through sun and wind control.

Many of the main rooms of the house in the sketch are located on the south side where they will be flooded with the warmth, both physical and psychological, of the winter sun. In New Mexico, where it is a rare day when the sun fails to shine, this can actually make a difference in your heating bill IF some provision is made to control heat loss through the windows at night.

A single pane of glass lets out ten times more warmth than an insulated wall. Thermopane or other double-pane windows tend to keep heat in once it has been trapped. Heavy draperies pulled over the windows at night also serve to retard the loss of heat. The small windows of the old adobes did prevent heat loss, but larger windows are necessary on the south in present-day adobes if the sun's heat is to be used.

There must be a nice balance here between design and utility. The larger windows must blend harmoniously with the architecture of the house. Some provisions may have to be made for privacy when the house has been opened to the sun. If fixed sash is used, some form of ventilation will be necessary. This might be provided by auxiliary double-hung windows or by adjustable louvered openings below or beside the windows.

Turning the longest dimension of the house toward the south will mean that more rooms are exposed to the warmth of the winter sun heating the outside walls and slowing loss of heat from the house to the outside air. Try to locate the kitchen and living areas where they can benefit from it. Children's bedrooms, if they are used for study and play areas, might also benefit from this exposure. It is not so crucial for bedrooms which are used primarily as sleeping rooms and are lived in but little during the day.

It is pleasant to live in rooms warm with winter sunlight, but it is not always possible to orient your home to take advantage of it. The sun might be cut off by neighboring buildings. Your view might lie in another direction. Many artists and craftsmen prefer the north light in their studios because it is more constant. Some designers favor a northern exposure because the view to the north is pleasant, for objects are seen with full sunlight falling on them rather than shadow side to the viewer as they are seen through south windows.

It may still be possible to take some advantage of the sun's heat in winter in these rooms by using clerestory or high monitor windows which are elevated above the roof of the rest of the house and face south. They should be installed with movable sash so that they may be opened to drain off hot air which rises to the ceiling in summer and provided with an overhang to protect them from the sun's hot rays during that season.

If you plan to cash in on this dividend of solar heat, you must plan your heating system with this in mind. It may be wise to divide the house into two or more heating zones controlled by separate thermostats.

It is also possible to collect and store solar energy for use in a primary heating system.

MIT built its first solar house in 1939. Peter van Dresser, a pioneer in designing solar houses, had a solar house in Santa Fe in the 1950's. However, not much thought was given to incorporating solar heating into houses by the average home builder or home owner until there was an explosion of interest in the 1970s and 1980s brought about by the energy crisis. Government at both the national and state

House designed by Lyle Thompson has double walls of stabilized adobe bricks which need no other exterior finish. Seven large double glazed arched windows frame view of Ortiz Mountains as they open house to sun. Semicircular design of house exposes long south wall to sun, while curved north side is nestled into a south facing hillside. Thirteen skylights and five clerestory windows make interior bright. Back up heat is provided by four fireplaces and electric baseboards with separate thermostats.

Although this wall of the DeWerd home faces east, a similar window on a south wall would be a good passive solar collector. A small overhang would protect it from the summer sun.

Interior view of windows above showing detail of canvas shades installed to control light and reduce heat loss through the windows at night.

Orban home in Cedar Crest, New Mexico has 2 levels of large south-facing windows to bring warmth of sun inside. Wings have flat roofs. Steep corrugated roof on central section, while not a solar collector, suggests an attractive way to incorporate one.

Greenhouses attached to experimental house at Ghost Ranch, Abiqui. Greenhouse collects sun's heat which is stored in adobe walls and water-filled drums. Warm air rises, entering house through vents at ceiling. Cooled air drops to floor and returns to greenhouse via vents at the floor by natural convection.

Adobe by Rational Alternatives was designed and oriented for passive solar heating. Site gives privacy. Louvered openings permit circulation of air. Wooden louvers are attractive but do require maintenance. Whiteford home, Santa Fe.

"Sun sponge" designed by Steve Baer. The Church adobe in Corrales stores heat in water filled drums in south facing windows. Plastic covered greenhouse also collects solar heat. Wall is painted white behind solar water heater (left of two story windows) to reflect heat to it.

Former Balcomb home in First Village, Santa Fe, New Mexico combines good solar design with pleasing exterior. House is wrapped around 400 square feet of double glazed greenhouse facing south. Sun's heat is stored in 14″ thick adobe wall between greenhouse and house proper, passing into house with a ten hour lag. Small fans draw heated greenhouse air into rock storage bins located under floors of living room and dining room. Bins are 2 feet deep, ten feet wide and 19 feet long for one bin and fifteen feet long for the other. The adobe wall is shaded in summer by a balcony and the roof. Warm air is drawn off through vent visible above roof.

Solar adobe in Las Lunas, New Mexico was planned by owners with help of contractor. Living room, study, and master bedroom suite are located on south side of the house. An integrated greenhouse and large windows welcome winter sun. Clerestory windows allow sun to strike adobe walls of north wing where fenestration is minimal. Solar gain is estimated to be 80-85% of heating requirements. Solar collection blends with house which presents a traditional facade on three sides.

Santa Fe home designed by Stephen C. Merdler has clerestories and south facing window walls.

Slanting windows in the solarium of the Los Lunas adobe collect solar heat.
Projecting rafters will support an "eyebrow" to shade the glass in summer.

Trombe wall, First Village, Santa Fe. Heat is collected by pre-cast concrete
sections filled with water and located behind south facing windows seen here.
Reflective surface in front increases heat collection. Entire reflective panel
can be raised to prevent heat loss through the windows at night while heat
from the trombe wall is slowly released into the living area.

Built-in planter runs the width of a sunny south wall in the dining room of a house designed and built by Lyle Thompson.

levels began to underwrite research and development and to encourage the use of solar heating by giving tax rebates and the like.

American technology was focused primarily on developing a heating system which maintained the constant thermostatically controlled heat that everyone was used to. Complex systems were designed with collectors that heated air or a liquid which then flowed through pipes or radiators or through storage materials such as gravels, salts, or water from which heat could be extracted. Houses began to sprout roof collectors in elaborate arrays. These systems were expensive to build and install and difficult to maintain. In some instances the costs proved to be more than the projected savings.

In the meantime, architects primarily in California, Arizona and New Mexico began to design houses with low cost low technology passive solar systems, using the house walls themselves for storage. While adobe is not a very good insulator, its mass makes it outstanding for saving heat. Some interesting adobe houses were designed with integral greenhouses, trombe walls, direct gain windows or convection systems which employed the fact that air rises when warm and sinks when cooled.

Los Alamos and Sandia Laboratories did extensive studies of low impact solutions. As more and more houses were built, a body of data and personal experience was developed which can help those who wish to design their own passive systems. The list of publications at the end of this chapter includes information from extremely technical to seat-of-the-pants practical.

In our sunny Southwest it surely makes sense to tap this free, renewable, nonpolluting and readily available energy together with a local building material to build passive solar heated adobe houses. This is especially appealing to do-it-yourselfers looking for low cost solutions. "Home grown" solar adobes perform very satisfactorily. Architect designed homes may be more sophisticated, but either can be aesthetically appealing and kind to the environment.

The "sun sponge" designed by Steve Baer (see photograph on p. 30) is a good example of direct gain collection. Sun pouring in the south windows warms the air and is soaked up by the floor, the adobe walls and bancos, and water-filled fifty gallon drums. At night the stored heat is slowly released, evening out temperature swings, while insulated shutters, the patented bead walls, or heavy draperies keep the heat from escaping through the windows. In Albuquerque it was found that single glazing with good insulation at night out-performed double glazing without insulation. Overhangs and shades control the amount of heat which is admitted to the house in autumn, late spring and summer.

Heat control is an important consideration when you plan direct gain collection. Tilted windows do maximize gain in winter, but overheating is difficult to control with overhangs, eye brows and other devices. For that reason upright glazing is now recommended.

Sun filled rooms can be very pleasant. However some people may object to the glare and the fading of fabrics and furniture. In city neighborhoods opening the house to the sun could mean a loss of privacy. A structure or landscaping added later by a neighbor could cut off or reduce the amount of sun striking direct gain windows.

The State of New Mexico has a solar rights act which allows you to file a claim to solar rights. A homeowner who is the first to use his solar rights can prevent a neighbor from putting up new buildings or additions or planting trees which keep the sun from reaching his collector. Investigate your solar rights if you live in other states.

David Wright compares a small well insulated house designed to trap and hold the sun's heat to a thermos bottle.

Large houses can also use solar heat effectively because there is less exterior wall for the inside volume. Large houses may have a better flywheel effect. Their mass keeps temperature variations at a tolerable level.

Berming or putting the house into a south facing hillside, when possible, will reduce heat loss from the outside walls, but hillside construction can be expensive.

Passive heated houses do experience temperature swings, but in my experience they have not been a problem. There is a morning lag but a sweater is often all that is needed to make one comfortable. Backup heating is used for those days when there is no solar heat collection. It always surprises me how much heat a greenhouse can collect even on an overcast day.

The original owners spent a minimum of five hours a week tending the greenhouse garden in House #1 of First Village near Santa Fe. (See photograph on page 31.) Dedicated gardeners who raise flowers and vegetables for the table could spend much more. The flooring, house wall, water-filled drums, soil, and even the plants themselves can modify greenhouse temperatures. For some owners a greenhouse may be merely a sun spot and a direct gain collector for solar heat which is moved into the living quarters.

Heat from our solar greenhouse is pumped directly into the house by a fan and a convective loop through windows and a door. In summer, late spring and early fall overheating is controlled by opening the sliding glass doors which make up the south wall. Wind turbines on the roof exhaust the hot air. A removable bamboo screen made of bamboo fencing is attached to the roof rafters under the glazing to further cut out the sun in summer. Overheating can also be controlled by shutting the greenhouse off from the rest of the house. Integral greenhouses require more sophisticated controls for overheating.

Greenhouses are one of the best and cheapest retrofits for adobe houses with a long wall exposed to the south sun. In addition to solar gain, by serving as a buffer for wind and cold they reduce heat loss from the house. Another practical retrofit is the trombe wall.

A trombe wall collector uses the house wall itself to store heat. The sun, passing through double glazed glass, warms the wall and the cavity between the glass and the wall. To increase collection the adobe wall is painted or stained black or a very dark color. Heated air rises in the cavity and enters the house through upper vents. As the air cools in the house it sinks to the floor and flows back into the collector through lower vents which have dampers and are located slightly above floor level so cold air won't flow back into the house on cloudy days. The heat stored in the adobe wall also radiates into the house. A reflective surface is used to further increase heat gain.

Take note that as air circulates through the cavity it is hard to keep dust put and there is no access to the space to clean it. If the vents do not have dampers, cool air will enter the house at night so the vents must be closed manually.

Another passive system uses rock bin storage for heat pumped from roof or other collectors. This requires a fan to move hot air from the collector into and through the rocks. The heat is then released from the bin at night or on cloudy days when the air flow from the rocks is reversed. Riverbed rocks four to six inches in diameter are a good size. Uniform size is important to avoid having small rocks filling in spaces between the larger rocks and impeding air flow through them. A short flat rock bed is better than a long skinny bed. There is an optimum size for the amount of rock storage, although increasing this amount does not substantially affect the effectiveness of the system.

Peter van Dresser designed a sun dwelling in El Rito, New Mexico which stored heat from a corrugated galvanized steel roof constructed as a collector. This house was also interesting because it used exposure to the night sky as a cooling device for a food storage area. Mr. van Dresser said that a common mistake in designing rock storage is overkill in the amount of storage planned. While not critical in terms of solar heat storage, it does cost in space and labor. The amateur builder may also be tempted to overdesign the collectors of a passive system.

Passive solar systems have many advantages: no moving parts, low maintenance, no noise, use of common and easily available materials. On the minus side, there is slow warming up time, inability to store enough heat for prolonged cloudy periods and a tendency to air pollution in houses well insulated and air tight. More interaction is required by the homeowner who must insulate windows at night, exhaust hot air when there is overheating and supplement the system with backup heating in cloudy weather.

In the summer the angle of the sun's rays will be different from the winter angle. A four to six foot overhang will usually be sufficent to keep the rays from striking south windows when they are not wanted.

There are various methods for determining just exactly how much overhang or porch roof will be needed to deflect the rays of the sun from house walls and windows during the summer and yet allow the maximum entry of the sun's rays in winter. Several quite technical methods are treated in Aaronin's *Climate and Architecture.* You must plot the point at which the angle of the sun's rays will be intercepted by the overhang in both winter and summer. This angle varies with the latitude. In New Mexico it varies from about 32 degrees on December 22 to roughly 76 degrees on June 22. Ideally the sun should not enter the windows until September and should not touch the house walls much after the end of April. The amount of overhang will vary with its height above the windows and its pitch, if any.

The south windows may also be protected by a sunshade such as a deciduous vine on a trellis which will provide the desired shade in summer but will not intercept the sun in winter. A grape arbor constructed of heavy posts and *vigas* will look effective with pueblo type adobes and provide architectural interest as well as a pleasant outdoor sitting area in summer.

Every home builder in New Mexico could reap real benefits from the proper orientation of the structure with respect to the sun, not only because he could take advantage of the warmth of the winter sun but because he could control the heat and glare during our hot summers as well. Since the hot rays of the low late afternoon sun are difficult to keep out of the house, windows on the west side might well be kept at a minimum or eliminated entirely. Carports and garages located on the west act as buffers to the sun's heat. The shade of any existing trees should be utilized to the fullest extent by the way in which the house is placed. Dense shade from trees can reduce the summer temperatures in your house by as much as twenty degrees.

Trees are especially valuable when they are tall enough to shade the roof. Heat radiated from the roof can make an appreciable difference in inside temperatures in summer. Don't think that those thick adobe walls will keep you cool in summer or warm in winter if the roof is poorly insulated. Good roof insulation is a must for comfort.

Early builders in New Mexico depended upon a thick layer of dirt for insulation. Even the grass and tumbleweeds which used to sprout on the thick earthen roofs of the old adobes actually served some practical purpose. Grass roofs are now being used by architects in Mexico and elsewhere to prevent excessive roof temperatures. Pitched roofs, if a way is provided to draw hot air out of the attic space, are generally cooler than flat roofs. White or light roofs will be cooler than a nonreflective black roof.

Surrounding your house with a pool of shade from porches and plantings can greatly increase summer comfort by preventing the reflection of heat and sun glare into the house windows and by shading the walls, which would otherwise absorb heat. Good orientation, supplemented by good design for adequate sun control, can materially increase both your comfort and your pleasure in your house and the grounds about it.

The wind also affects comfort. You seek the breeze in summer because it cools you. You invite this cooling effect by planning for cross ventilation in your rooms. You are aware that the wind on a winter day can greatly increase your discomfort. The wind does not lower the air temperature about you but does lower the comfort index. When it is seventy degrees, a breeze of eight miles per hour will cool you as much as if the temperature had dropped twelve degrees. It may be shirt sleeves weather at only fifty degrees if you are sitting in the sun and there is no wind. It is the power of the wind to cool surfaces that makes it affect our comfort. Minneapolis Honeywell states in a brochure that when the outside temperature is thirty degrees with the wind at thirty miles an hour, a heat loss on the windy side of the building is the same as if the outside temperature were only four degrees.

Wind control cannot be too large a factor in the orientation of a house on a city lot, since in the city the wind is deflected and broken up into turbulent areas by surrounding trees and buildings, but each of us can use individual solutions to protect outdoor living areas from wind. This is discussed in the chapter on landscaping. You may find that full length windows with movable sash are undesirable in areas where the sand blows because of this eddying and turbulence.

In rural areas, prevailing winds should be taken into account. You may place the narrow end of the house toward the prevailing winds. Small windows or a closed facade on the windward side will help to prevent heat loss. The planting of hedge rows as a wind control device can supply a good measure of protection. In locating houses in mountainous areas, you should keep in mind the tendency of air to flow downhill like water. Cold air tends to flow downhill and to collect in pools behind natural barriers and in hollows and valleys.

Just as in sun control, planning for wind control means an integration of orientation, the design of the house, and the landscaping. The house and grounds should be planned as a unit. This is site utilization in its fullest sense.

Luckily, good site utilization is more a matter of good planning than of a large budget, although a small budget will limit some solutions. Here are some money saving ideas to keep in mind when you place your house on the site. A kitchen to the front of a city lot will mean savings in running sewer and gas lines. Locating the kitchen, bathrooms, and utility area close together in a core so that plumbing

Wooden steps to a second-story bedroom are cantilevered from the two-story-high circular stone unit containing three fireplaces which forms the core of the Friedman adobe in Nambe. Sand cast mantel, exposed aggregate hearth, rough-sawn paneling, and unfinished stabilized adobe walls blend in an interplay of textures which might be overpowering in a small house but is very pleasing here in an open plan with large rooms and a high ceiling.

Conversation corner of open kitchen in the Gale residence. Sliding doors hide efficient pantry shelves. Hanging pots brighten white adobe walls. Designer, Nat Kaplan.

Mexican tile dado brightens the kitchen of the fine old adobe restored by the Lienaus in Sandoval.

Knotty pine and Mexican tile decorate the attractive kitchen of the Marshall Armijo adobe. No attempt has been made to carry storage space to the high ceiling.

Handsome dish storage unit is set into the adobe wall in the Lienau kitchen. Doors were carved by the owner.

Everything is within reach in the efficient small kitchen of the Witherspoon home.

Simple hanging shelf could be adapted for kitchen storage.

Carved doors enhance a storage unit with a pass-through separating the kitchen from the dining area. McKee home, Sandoval.

Built-in shelves in the Witherspoon home. Simple chip carving and spindles add regional flavor.

Strong horizontal line of bookshelves and high windows are pleasing in large, high-ceilinged livingroom. Epperson home, Corrales.

Handsome iron staircase silhouetted against stark white adobe wall lends drama to the interior of adobe designed by Hap Crawford.

Small planter brightens an entry hall. Partial divider makes a visual separation of the hall from the living room. Hap Crawford, designer.

Stove, barbecue, chopping block line up on one side of corridor kitchen.

Front entry of the Friedman home showing the play of texture on texture of rough-sawn stained wood siding, unpainted stabilized adobe walls, caramel colored ceramic floor tile, stained glass windows.

Trio of old
doors used in
restored adobes.
Miller,
Krogdahl,
Knight homes.

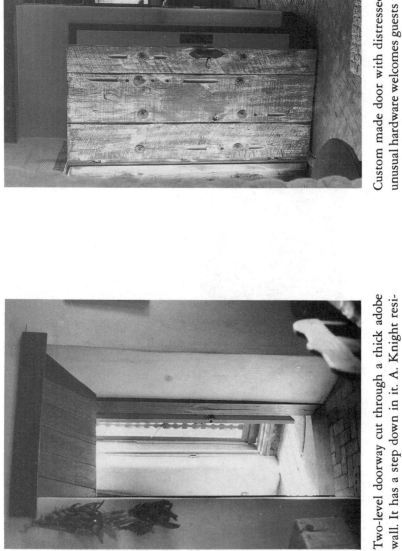

Custom made door with distressed finish and unusual hardware welcomes guests to Gale residence. Nat Kaplan, designer.

Two-level doorway cut through a thick adobe wall. It has a step down in it. A. Knight residence.

Antique doors from Mexico are used at front entrance to Cummings adobe,
Albuquerque.

Rough-sawn lumber, Mexican iron light fixture, and heavy carved door blend with unplastered stabilized adobe bricks in a contemporary treatment. Joe Priestley, H. L. Cleff.

Custom built door blends well with simple territorial.

Streetside entranceway opens into a small entrance court with high adobe walls to preserve privacy. P. G. McHenry, builder.

Deeply recessed entry of Witherspoon home. Green glass bottles are set into brickwork surrounding the door.

Accessories with a southwestern flavor draw attention to the door of the guest house at the Shreve home, Albuquerque.

Handsome contemporary treatment and a simple planting of Santolina welcome guests to the Casteel home.

Double doors open into a diminutive entry garden. Treatment is plain but dramatic. Tappan home, Sandoval.

Small recessed entry porch protects guests, adds architectural interest to a simple adobe.

Handsome entry designed by Nat Kaplan.

Deep recess protects entry door at deWerd home, Corrales. Walls were laid up straight and arch was constructed later of lathe and wire before plastering.

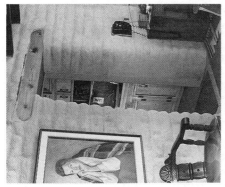

Archway in Gifford home, Corrales, has soft irregular contours built out with mud. Wall was covered with a number of coats of plaster when the house was acquired. Brick outlines were drawn on the wall and cut into it with a hand tool. A roll of wire mesh which would fit comfortably into the hand was used to deepen and round the grooves before the wall was given finish coat. A similar effect can be obtained in a new wall built of adobes made of slightly soft mix from which the form was lifted as soon as they were poured allowing the sides to slump slightly. Mortar joints are struck with a special rounded tool. The wall can then be finished with dry wall texture.

Antique doors from Mexico have movable center panel. Home of Mr. and Mrs. Jan Cummings, Albuquerque.

Unusual window of indeterminate age in an old adobe in Bernallilo.

Red pepper string, shocking pink iron work at the Shreve's front door, Albuquerque.

Elaborate window trim is focal point of a mud-plastered wall. A. Knight residence, Albuquerque.

Interesting treatment of a small, high window, Krogdahl's, Sandoval.

Bright print gathered onto a metal frame dresses a deep window at the home of Mr. and Mrs. Paul Taylor, Mesilla.

Deep window sills of Los Luceros are utilized to display art objects from the extensive collection of Mr. and Mrs. Charles Collier. Walls of the lower story of the house are of puddled adobe four feet thick. In modern adobes a similar effect could be obtained by building closets around window. Note how carving on lintel dresses curtainless window.

Small window is enhanced by a simple grille made by the owner. Sandoval adobe.

One-hundred-year-old grilles cover tall windows and give an air of great elegance to the roadside facade of the deWerd adobe, Corrales.

Friedman home in Nambe. Roof spirals around two-story-high central section. House is constructed of stabilized adobe bricks made on the site.

Small adobe guest house at the Juan Jose Prada house, Santa Fe.

Traditional adobe with a native planting. Rose home, Corrales.

Old and new wings have been blended into a harmonious whole. Krogdahl residence, Sandoval.

White plaster draws attention to the entry of the Utton home, Sandoval.

Old and new wings enclose a walled garden. Kimmons, Corrales.

Plain streetside facade at El Zaguan, Santa Fe, gives no hint of the secluded inner garden, reportedly laid out by Adolph Bandelier.

Main house. Williams Ranch, Pojoaque.

Rogers adobe, Albuquerque.

Home of Mr. and Mrs. D. B. Dunlap, Corrales. Sandy Root, designer and builder.

One-story home of stabilized adobe with a "burnt" adobe coping.

Stabilized adobe walls have a strong shadow line. Eyebrow protects sliding door to patio. High wall gives privacy. Nat Kaplan, designer.

Eastman home, Albuquerque. Garden walls enclose outdoor living space, increase the apparent size of the house, adding architectural interest.

is concentrated means a savings. Locating the garage or carport to the front saves the expense of a long driveway.

Corners cost money. A square house or one which is a simple rectangle will cost less to build than that H-shaped rambler. Weigh the advantages you will gain from an L, H, U, or Y shape against your budget. The cheapest solution could be expensive in the long run if you sacrifice comfort, utility, and the full use of your site for economies which will represent but a part of your total investment. Your aim is the most functional house you can get for that investment. You want to live high for the bottom dollar. Happily even the most rigid budget does not exclude original and creative solutions and may indeed stimulate them.

You might plan to eliminate some interior partitions which cost in space as well as for their construction. The greatest savings will lie in doing some of the work of building yourself. Cutting the number of square feet to be built does not save as much as you would suppose, because the big expenses such as those for heating and plumbing still remain fairly constant. Ways to save will be pointed out as we consider each room of the house and how it can be planned to bring bigger dividends of good living.

As you study your plot plan and the various ways in which a house could be placed upon it, you will arrive at some conception of the shape that the house must take. Your next problem will be room arrangement within that framework. Here again a variety of choices will be open to you.

One of the best ways to begin is to study books and magazines which contain house plans. Try to visualize your family moving through the rooms as you study them. Study the traffic patterns and the provisions for privacy. You may want a bedroom wing which is isolated from the rest of the house for quiet and privacy. You may admire an open plan in which the living space flows together. You may reject some kitchens as too large, some bedrooms as too small.

Gradually you will begin to see a pattern in your preferences, and the type of room arrangement you like will begin to emerge. Jot down features that particularly appeal to you. This is the time to make lists. Even if you plan to leave the design to an architect you can help him by deciding what you like and the room arrangement you prefer.

He will want to know the number of rooms you want, their size, the number of baths, the sort of equipment you want in the kitchen, special storage requirements, and special provisions which must be made for family hobbies such as a dark room or a built-in hi-fi. He will ask what furniture you have and what you plan to buy in the future. He should know whether you prefer modern or traditional or transitional. The number of family members, the ages of the children, the number of the family who work, the use of outside help for cleaning or gardening or cooking will all have bearing on the final plan.

The house must be designed to fit your pattern of family living. Do you entertain often or rarely? Casually or formally? Does your family like to eat in the kitchen? Are there traffic tangles in the bathroom every morning? Must there be a spot where someone can practice on the tuba or the drums? Does father work at home? Is home office space needed? All of these requirements can be provided for with intelligent planning; yet the final result need not be so individual that resale would be difficult.

Let me assure you that this extra thought and planning are worth while. A good custom house is like a custom tailored suit: it fits! There are too many little day by day irritations in a house that does not. Maybe it is too little storage or too much of the wrong kind, too many steps to the refrigerator, too much traffic through the living room, lack of formal dining room or the presence of one which wastes space, too many people queued up before the bathroom in the morning. No one has ever built the perfect house, but good planning means good living and a far better return for your investment.

During your research you have probably come upon a floor plan which suggests an arrangement you like. There is a relationship between the living area, the bedroom area, and the kitchen-utility area that you find workable in relation to your needs. If its size and shape will roughly conform to your site, you may want to use this as the beginning of your plan. If you are still looking for the ideal arrangement, draw various combinations of three rough circles, each representing one of these three areas until some arrangement seems good. Try the kitchen in front for economy, the bedroom wing to the rear for privacy and quiet, or perhaps group the kitchen, utility room, and baths in a core surrounded by the rest of the rooms. When some doodle pleases you draw it roughly to scale to see if it will fit your site.

It is usually wise to plan for a separate entry and for access to some parts of the house without crossing others. Except in unusual circumstances it is not desirable to cross one bedroom to reach another. Bathrooms located between two bedrooms with an entrance to each were thought to be poor planning several years ago. Now the trend toward compartmented bathrooms has largely removed this objection. The kitchen should be close to the dining area for easy serving. The utility area may be located in the bedroom wing to save steps, for most of the soiled laundry must be carried from this part of the house and clean clothing returned to it. One objection to this will be the noise made by the laundry equipment if there is someone in the family who sleeps late or small children who nap.

Halls and corridors create privacy and allow a house to ramble, but they can waste much valuable space. Strict economy may dictate the omission of hall space in your plan. Hallways can sometimes be put to use by devoting the walls to storage units. A corridor might be widened to serve as a sitting or play room. Early adobes sometimes had a *sala* which doubled as an entrance hall and a reception or ballroom and gave access to rooms opening off both sides.

If you plan to build a more or less traditional style of adobe, any fairly standard room size and arrangement will be quite satisfactory. However, if your plan calls for large openings in the walls, a very open plan with few partitions, extremely high ceilings, or a second story, be sure you understand the limitations of adobe and the construction processes needed so that you can plan within the structural limits of the material.

If you arrive at an arrangement which seems satisfactory, your next step is to fit the various rooms into that space. Can you fit into it all the equipment and features you want?

Perhaps the most critical room in this respect is the kitchen, which is by the way, the most expensive room in the house. It is also one area in which a great deal of a family's time is spent, an average of five hours a day. The big objectives in kitchen design will be the saving of labor and getting your money's worth from that expensive equipment.

A great deal of attention has been given to the development of a labor-saving shape for kitchens. The number of steps between appliances has been tabulated, and time and motion studies have been made. Actually an extra step or two is not going to be a critical matter to anyone in good shape, and some people, especially those with large families where there may be several cooks in the kitchen at once, like a large kitchen with generous spaces between appliances.

Appliances are generally grouped in counter arrangements which are U-shaped, L-shaped, or consist of two parallel counters. This corridor kitchen utilizes a small space well but can be inconvenient if the family is large and traffic is channeled through the kitchen, because traffic must pass through the work area. The U is considered the most desirable. If the distance across the U is not too great, it is a convenient arrangement in which the work area can be kept out of the traffic pattern. Four feet across the U is probably the minimum requirement for space. Six feet is better. An island sink or range may be used to place appliances conveniently close to each other in a large kitchen.

In placing appliances, remember which way your refrigerator door opens. Be sure that there is enough counter space for a landing spot fifteen inches wide beside the range and refrigerator. No doors should open into the kitchen where they will interfere with anyone working at the appliances.

It is not necessary to place the cooking top and a built-in oven side by side. Separate units allow flexible arrangements. For economy of space, however, a unit which combines the cooktop and oven will usually be more practical. A dishwasher should be located beside the sink because they are plumbed together and because labor is saved when dishes are rinsed and placed in the dishwasher without extra motions. The disposal unit, which flushes away food as it is rinsed from the dishes, is also a labor-saving member of this team. To save counter space consider a small single sink rather than a double one if you have a dishwasher. The stainless steel sink is no longer an expensive luxury and is my personal preference.

You would be wise to draw the space you have allotted to the kitchen to scale, using one quarter inch to each foot of measurement and then draw a line to represent the tops of the counters to see how much counter space you will have and how much will be taken up by the appliances.

Nine lineal feet of counter space is about minimum. Figure that a double sink will take about thirty-two inches, a range top thirty to thirty-six inches, a built-in oven about two feet. The dishwasher will take up two feet of under counter space. Allow a generous three feet for a refrigerator. Don't forget to locate the door and window openings. An outside door is usually three feet wide. Inside doors are thirty or thirty-two inches wide.

The average counter top extends two feet out from the wall and is thirty-six inches from the floor. Mixing counters are thirty-two inches high. Pull-out boards are located at table top height, about thirty inches. Allow thirty inches minimum of work space at each side of the sink. A mixing counter will need about three feet of space.

The cabinets over the counter extend thirteen inches from the wall and begin about fifteen inches from the counter top. Anything over eighty-seven inches from the floor will be useful only for storing items rarely used. This space may be furred out to the ceiling instead of devoted to cupboards. You will need about twelve square feet of storage space for glasses and china and six square feet per member of the family for general storage.

Use adjustable shelving or plan for items which are tall. Be sure you have a place for the Post Toasties and for tall stemware. A shallow shelf six inches deep placed above the bottom shelf in your baking cupboard will hold small boxes like gelatin and puddings and leave room beneath for staples. Revolving shelves installed in a deep corner will bring the contents of its shelves within easy reach and make that space function for the maximum storage and convenience. You may want slots for tray storage, divided drawers for silver, shallow shelves for platters, a built-in vegetable bin, or knife slots in a counter top to keep sharp knives within easy reach.

Plan storage by areas: a baking center, dish storage, and a place for staples and canned goods near the sink and range. Two-way dish storage with doors opening into the kitchen and the dining room will simplify the setting of the table at meal time and make it easy to return clean dishes to the cupboard from the kitchen side, close to the sink or dishwasher.

A recent trend in kitchen storage is the return of the pantry in the form of a closet with well-planned shelving that will accommodate bulk storage items, canned goods, and supplies all within easy reach and sight. Floor-to-ceiling storage like this behind one door can be both a space saver and a saving of fussy cabinet work. Carry this a step further and place a compact kitchen with open shelves behind a pair of folding doors or place the mixing center with its bulky supplies all within reach on open shelves behind a sliding door hung on barn-door hardware.

In a very small kitchen where swinging cupboard doors will not be practical, a pantry at one end might supply the answer to storage needs. Hang pots and pans over the stove and place often used items on shallow open shelves near the point of use. You might like hanging shelves made of rough lumber and supported by ropes from the ceiling in the kitchen of a rustic adobe.

The more specialized storage you plan for, the more expensive your cabinets will be to construct. Many custom features can now be found in prefabricated units which may be purchased, assembled or ready for assembly, in a variety of materials and finishes and in so many sizes that a custom installation is possible in almost any kitchen.

While you are planning, keep in mind extras that it would be nice to have:

> telephone jack
> ventilating fan
> built-in appliance center for mixer, juicer, and blender
> chopping block
> racks for wine storage
> built-in refrigerator which may be hung or installed
>   under counter
> outlet for kitchen clock
> kitchen desk
> kitchen barbecue

The indoor barbecue may be gas-fired or heated with charcoal or electrically heated ceramic coals. A barbecue and a cooking unit are often installed side by side under the same ventilating hood. The usual kitchen ventilating unit is not adequate for a barbecue using gas or charcoal.

The indoor barbecue has probably become increasingly popular because of the development of the family kitchen or family room for casual family living and entertaining. The fireplace is often located here rather than in a formal living room. The emphasis is on informal furnishings and easy-care surfaces. Often the family eats here. It is either frankly a part of the kitchen or the kitchen is adjacent to it, often separated from it only by a counter. Kitchen colors and kitchen cabinet woods are correlated to its decor. In open plans, the living room, family room, and kitchen may flow together with little separation. This increases the illusion of spaciousness. It does have its drawbacks, however, for noise and cooking odors cannot be shut away. Even acoustical ceilings and ventilating fans will not completely control them. Not everyone will mind, but if you are one who does you should consider this possibility while you are in the planning process.

General lighting in the kitchen is usually supplemented by direct lighting over the cooking unit and the sink. Do not forget an adequate number of electric outlets, located for the greatest convenience. Think where you will be using the mixer, the toaster, the electric can opener. Remember that you will need a 240-V outlet for the electric stove and the electric water heater.

Locating the water heater near the kitchen and utility area will mean a savings. Long runs mean a long time before water runs hot from the faucet. An electric booster pump can be installed to correct this, but it costs to install and operate it. Hot water pipes should be insulated.

Gas water heaters placed inside the house may be a hazard. They are often installed in a garage or heater room with an outside entrance. Leaking water heaters and washing machines may damage flooring or carpets if located in the living area. A brick or a cement floor with a drain in the utility area will remove this problem.

Kitchen flooring should be durable and easy to clean. Some prefer resilient flooring such as linoleum, cork, vinyl, or asphalt tile. They can be had in various guages. Cork tile will bleach in the sun and may show grease spatters. Asphalt tile also shows grease spots. Brick flooring is often used throughout an adobe house. When it is well sealed, it can be grease resistant. It is fireproof and withstands hard usage. It supplies decorative interest because of its color and texture. Highly waxed floors of brick do show footprints and dust easily, however.

Brick floors on grade save over floors which require a sub floor covered with other materials, especially if they are installed by the owner's labor. Natural materials like brick require only a simple finish and are not hard to maintain.

Counter tops can also add color and textural interest to the kitchen decor. Linoleum and vinyl are commonly used, but in adobe houses Mexican tiles, hard-fired brick, patio tile, laminated counters of hardwood strips, or mosaic would all be appropriate. Some form of splash board for splash and spatter protection is a good idea behind the sink and the cooking surface.

The washer and dryer are sometimes installed in the kitchen. Location in the kitchen means that the plumbing is grouped. Kitchen floor and counter surfaces are generally waterproof. They may also be located in a bathroom, a hall, in a bedroom wing, or in a closet with folding doors. Allow at least five feet for a washer and dryer installed side by side. Gas dryers must be vented. It is a general practice to vent all dryers to the outside. An electric dryer will require a 240-V outlet.

Do have a utility room if you can afford it. Room for sorting clothes and setting up the ironing board close to the dryer is a real convenience. The freezer could be located here. A separate burner and a small sink would make canning and freezing garden produce convenient. It is a good place for the sewing machine and could be used as a hobby room. It might double as a dark room or a small home office. A well-planned utility room will certainly not be a waste of the space allotted to it.

Now that it has become easy to get financing for a house with an inside bathroom, the kitchen, bath, and utility room core has come into its own and is used with increasing frequency in houses of all price ranges. Lighting diffused over a plastic ceiling, sky lights or clerestory windows will provide good illumination for inside bathrooms, better in fact than the small high windows of obscure glass which are so often installed in bathrooms.

A direct opposite of this trend toward the inside bathroom is the bath opened with large glass areas to its own private garden. This is not cheap, but it is nice to live with. It takes planning to secure adequate privacy and to keep the occupant of the bathroom from being chilled in the winter by the large expanse of glass. A compartmented bath will allow one to bathe in comfort away from the windows, while the dressing room with a built-in lavatory benefits from the light and the feeling of space that the window wall gives.

Dividing the bathroom into compartments extends the usefulness of the three-fixture bath by allowing more than one person to use it at one time. A tub or shower reached from two half baths, each containing a water closet and lavatory, gives almost the convenience of two full baths with one less fixture, plus the economy that comes from grouping the plumbing. This and a slight saving of space will be balanced, however, by the expense for extra partitions, doors, ventilating, and lighting fixtures.

An adequate bathroom can be installed in a space five feet by seven feet, four feet by eight feet, or even five feet by five feet. There is a trend toward larger and more attractive bathrooms. They are enhanced by colored fixtures, a variety of colors and patterns in vinyl and tile flooring, the handsome vanities which are now available ready to install or which can be custom built, washable wallpapers, mirrored walls, sunken tubs, and wall-to-wall carpeting.

The lavatory occasionally moves into the bedroom and may be installed in a cabinet styled like a fine piece of furniture. Bathrooms and dressing rooms are often combined. A wardrobe closet may be located between the bedroom and bath so that it opens from both sides. The chief objection to this is the control of bathroom noises. Contrary to popular belief, closets do not make good devices for insulating a bedroom from noise.

Often a bedroom and its adjoining bath are decorated as a suite with the same color scheme. In striving to avoid the sterile look of the bathroom of bygone years we may sometimes lose sight of the fact that bathroom surfaces must be easy to keep clean and sanitary and must withstand the effects of splashing and steam. Durable surfaces, good lighting, and enough space to use each fixture comfortably should be the prime considerations. To prevent bathroom accidents, do not use floor surfaces that become slippery when wet. Do not place the electric outlets near the tub or shower. Install a grab bar by the bath tub. Make some provision for the storage of medicines out of reach of small children.

There are many ways in which fixtures may be placed. To make the best use of bathroom space, draw the outlines of the room to scale and sketch in various arrangements, or cut little pieces of paper the proper size for each fixture and move them about until an arrangement looks good. Plumbing fixtures come in any number of sizes and shapes. Each manufacturer puts out a brochure and catalogs listing the size of various items in his line. You can use the following measurements as a rough guide.

The recessed tub is usually five feet long and twenty-nine to thirty-one inches wide. A corner tub is five feet long by thirty-one inches. A square tub comes four feet square or in assorted smaller sizes. Lavatories are usually about twenty inches wide and project fifteen to seventeen inches from the wall. Counters with built-in lavatories should be about two feet deep. They should be at least three feet wide. Toilets are twenty-one to twenty-four inches wide and project about two and a half feet. If you plan to install one in an alcove, the alcove should be about fifty-four inches long and thirty inches wide. Shower stalls should be three feet square. If space is at a premium, they can be placed across a corner. Allow space for towel bars and paper holders in convenient locations.

There is a real savings if pipes are concentrated and you put all three fixtures on one wall or, if the bathroom has partitions, around one stack. Colored fixtures cost a little more than white ones. White fixtures allow more freedom in planning color schemes and will not limit your choice of colors if you redecorate.

You can have bathroom layouts planned and order prefabricated plumbing from the mail order catalogs. If you install plumbing and plan to pour a slab floor, remember that it will be costly to repair or remodel the plumbing, because the slab will have to be torn up and repoured. Plan ahead for future expansion.

Here is a checklist of bathroom equipment it is nice to have:

> Shower head over bath tub (Even if you always use the shower, plan for one tub. FHA regulations require one.
> Ventilating fan (required by some building codes in each section of a compartmented bath)
> Ceiling fixture for radiant heating
> Booster pump for a long line from the hot water heater
> Glass shower door or tub enclosure
> Sun lamp
> Heated towel bars
> Bidet
> Walk-through shower with a sliding door to a swimming pool or sun garden
> Sunken bathing pool with radiantly heated tiles

Since you spend about one third of your life in it, the bedroom merits more attention than it often receives from the home builder.

In fact, the only requirement that is often voiced is that bedrooms be large in size; yet the difference between a good room and a poor one is how this square footage is used. For example, a room which is square or nearly so makes more efficient use of space than a long narrow room. Furniture arrangement may be inconvenient even in a large room if there is little uninterrupted wall space.

In some cases a large bedroom is a wise way to invest space. A bedroom-sitting room for the master bedroom gives parents a retreat when the children take over the living room. Large bedrooms are a convenience during illness or convalescence. To some people a bedroom represents a private retreat, a place to withdraw from the togetherness of this era of the family room and to quietly pursue personal interests and hobbies. The bedroom may provide a quiet corner for the home office and do double duty as a sewing room.

On the other hand, it is foolish to give over large areas of the total living space to big bedrooms and then close them off all winter to save heat. You must analyze your own needs. Today the bathdressing room often takes over one function of the bedroom and less space may be needed. The trend toward built-in chests, desks, and vanities also means less space may be required. Oversized and little used bedrooms are a luxury most of us cannot afford.

Large or small, the bedroom must be planned for comfort and convenience. Cross ventilation, wall space for the beds where they will not face the window, adequate closet space should be provided. If possible, the bedrooms should be isolated from street noise. The bedrooms of small children should not be located across the house from the master bedroom if mother is to hear them call at night.

Children's bedrooms are sometimes planned as dormitories or separated by folding screens so that a large play area may be opened up for their daytime activities. In actual practice, bedrooms of this type do not always function well. Although it is not a normal thing, illness must be considered in one's planning. Some provision must be made for the occasional isolation of a patient and for insuring quiet and light control to increase a sick child's comfort. The folding partition furnishes little actual privacy, and the arrangement is not very practical as children grow older. Many parents have planned for a children's play area only to find to their chagrin that the children prefer to play right under foot as they always have, close to mother and right in the center of anything interesting that might be going on.

There has been a tendency in recent years to dramatize the master bedroom. Many houses today have a master suite consisting of a bath-dressing room, bed-sitting room, and a private bedroom patio treated as an extension of the room. This can be both attractive and convenient yet need not be prohibitive in cost. Plan to utilize space well and to orient the bedroom properly. Since you borrow space from the outdoors, the bedroom need not be unduly large to seem luxurious. The bedroom garden must be landscaped so that it is pleasant to look at every month of the year and well screened for privacy. It must not trap heat and glare and reflect them back into the room in the summer.

A builder I know attributes his success in selling speculative houses to a very simple formula. He puts a large walk-in closet in every master bedroom. Plenty of storage is high on the list of what every buyer wants in his or her new home. A recent survey of home owners showed that, having been cramped as to closet space in a former home, they had gone overboard in demanding storage, storage, and more storage in a new one. But, this may surprise you, some found that they had actually ordered too much or at least too much of the wrong kind. You must have storage space to accommodate what you plan to put into it. The formula that storage areas should equal twelve per cent of the floor space in the living area does not insure you adequate space if you forget the bulkies like suitcases and do not plan special storage for hobby equipment and sporting goods.

The builder of speculative houses could not afford to pay for the cabinet work involved in building the banks of drawers, the cubby-holes for handbags, and the separate space for each pair of shoes in the beautifully organized closets one sees in the home planning magazines. An inexpensive gimmick or two would add to the storage space in a big closet. Two clothes rods could be installed, one over the other, on one side of a walk-in closet to accommodate blouses and suits. A narrow tier of adjustable shelves from floor to ceiling at the end of the closet would not be prohibitive in cost.

Bedroom closets often consist of a narrow wardrobe with folding doors across one end of the room. The minimum size for a wardrobe closet is twenty to twenty-four inches deep and six feet long. Occasionally wardrobes are divided into his and her units separated by a built-in vanity or a bed alcove.

Casework increases costs. Here is one way you might eliminate doors and casework for bedroom closets. A satisfactory closet, easy on the budget and on wall space can be made by a partial partition across one end of the room which screens the clothes rods and allows access at one end. This partition need extend only part way to the ceiling. It could be a decorative grill or a step down adobe wall that creates a corner for a tiny adobe fireplace. Linen storage should be located near the bedrooms and bathrooms. General storage could be tucked in beside a fireplace or line the wall of a long hall. Do not forget a broom closet, a guest closet near the front door, and built-in bookshelves.

You will find that many items could be stored in outside closets, perhaps in the garage or carport. Turning the carport sidewise to the street would hide the storage unit from the view of passersby.

Store items close to where they will be used. Store heavy things where they will not have to be lifted. Overhead storage can be inconvenient and actually downright dangerous if you must climb on something to reach it.

Even if outside storage is exploited to the fullest extent, the low, one-storied adobe without a basement or attic must give up a considerable amount of expensive interior floor space to storage. Plan to get the most you can from the space allotted to it.

Interior space is too expensive to be wasted in any manner. For this reason many people feel that a separate dining room which is used perhaps two hours a day and requires about one hundred forty square feet of floor space, is an extravagance they can ill afford. The dining alcove at one end of the living room has largely replaced it in homes of modest cost. Yet in the case of the disappearing dining room it may be wise to take a long look at your own requirements before ruling it out in your new home. By planning other uses for this space, you may be able to have your cake and eat in it, too.

The family room often doubles as a dining room, at least for family dining, a much better arrangement to my mind than coping with spills and crumbs on the wall-to-wall carpeting at one end of the living room. The ages of the children and the amount and fashion in which you entertain are factors you must consider in deciding your own requirements for a dining room.

The family room and living room are often located adjacent to each other so that large groups can be accommodated at parties. Having the one room open into the other in this manner does increase the feeling of space in a small house. Any time that you lessen the feeling of enclosure you gain an illusion of space.

A large entry hall patterned after the *sala* of earlier adobes, running the width of the house and giving access to all the rooms, would also give one this feeling of spaciousness. The total amount of hall space would probably be no more than the usual arrangement with a long bedroom hall. Architects sometimes make a small living room appear larger by opening it to an outside garden or an inside court. Both devices can add real touches of glamour. Large areas of glass add to the cost of the house, however.

The width of the house in early adobes was controlled to a large extent by the length of the *vigas* which were available. Today as you plan your house you should take into account the standard sizes of lumber and plan to use stock sash and doors to keep costs nominal.

As you sketch your plan to scale keep in mind that the thickness of adobe walls should be at least twelve inches if good insulation is desired. A 4x10x14 inch adobe brick should be laid up so that the wall is fourteen inches thick. Inside partitions will be about six inches wide if stud construction is used, or the width of your adobes if an adobe partition is planned. Adobe partitions use more of that expensive interior space but may be worth the additional expense. Thick walls and deep doorways add to the character of the rooms. They also provide good insulation against sound.

Some building codes will not allow adobe fireplaces. In some places two story adobes cannot be built. Wall heights may be regulated. Framing requirements will vary. These regulations are for your protection, but they are not uniform nor are they uniformly interpreted. What is acceptable in one place cannot be built in another, a source of much bewilderment to the amateur builder and much frustration to the professional. Nevertheless, the codes exist and you will be required to adhere to them.

It is going to take trial and error, arrangement and rearrangement to develop your house plan satisfactorily, yet this is time well spent. The success of the entire venture depends upon how well you do this step. A poor plan can produce nothing but a poor house no matter how carefully it may be built.

You want not only a good interior arrangement but also a pleasing appearance from the outside. Windows and doors must be located with an eye to the effect their placement will have on the exterior appearance of the house. Territorial houses often demand a formal balance of windows which are all the same size for the front facade.

Exterior trim should be in keeping with the architectural style of the house. Even the location of the plumbing affects the appearance of the house if vents or flues can be seen from the street. The fireplace chimney is often a pleasing element of exterior design.

The best way to see how your house will look is to draw elevations to scale. These are views of each side of the house showing the size and placement of windows and doors and other exterior details. You might find it fun to construct a scale model of light cardboard or of heavy craft paper. A pleasing exterior increases your pleasure in your home and also increases its resale value; yet many amateur home planners do not think of its importance until it is too late.

The adobe house derives much of its charm from the play of light and shadow on the gently irregular walls. The amateur may achieve by accident the character the professional architect achieves by design.

I have friends who built their adobe from a rough sketch drawn to scale. Several things in the finished house surprised them. Luckily they were happy surprises. Converting your sketch into actual working drawings will help you think through all the details of construction and to catch errors and omissions while they can still be corrected with an eraser. Working drawings are required with your application for a building permit. Your contractor will work from them. They show the exact location of every partition, closet, door, window, light plug, and plumbing fixture. The elevations show exactly how the finished house will look. Together with the list of specifications for the grade of lumber, type of wiring, kinds of equipment, and every bit of material that will go into the house, they spell out exactly what you expect.

If an architect draws your plans, he furnishes these for you. If you have been your own architect, you must have them drawn or do it yourself. The loan department of your bank or a building supply company can probably give you the name of draftsmen who can draw the final plans up for you. Contractors may supply the drawings if they have a design service. Engineering or architectural students at a local university might also draw them. The charge will vary, but a full set of working drawings takes many hours of work and will not be cheap, especially if several consultations are necessary to iron out wrinkles in your planning.

It is not too difficult to master the rudiments of blueprint drawing and to turn out an acceptable set of drawings yourself if you know something about construction and can be neat and patient. Any good book on blueprint drawing will give the standard symbols.

Reproductions of your drawings are not expensive. You will need sets for a contractor, subcontractors, and loan applications.

With the completion of the drawings, you may think that your planning has come to an end. However, planning is still needed to make the construction proceed smoothly and to secure decorating and landscaping which will make the finished house all that you had hoped for.

SUGGESTED READING

Dietz, Albert. *Dwelling House Construction,* 4th Edition. Cambridge: MIT Press, 1977.

Kern, Ken. *The Owner Built Home.* New York: Charles Scribners Sons, 1975.

Making the Adobe Brick. Berkley: 5th Street Press; distributed by Random House, 1971.

McHenry, P. G. *Adobe: Build It Yourself.* Univ. of Arizona Press, 1973.

Prowler, Donald. *Modest Mansions.* Emmanaus, PA: Rodale Press, 1985.

Stedman, Myrtle and Welfred. *Adobe Architecture.* Santa Fe: Suston Press, 1975.

For Solar:

Anderson, Bruce and Malcolm Wells. *Passive Solar Energy.* Andover, MA: Brick House Publishing, 1981.

Arizona Solar Energy Commission. *Arizona State Tours: A Guide Book to 1001 Solar Projects.* Phoenix, 1984.

Baer, Steve. *Sun Spots.* Mayne Island, B.C.: Cloudburst Press.

Bainbridge, David. *The First and Second Passive Solar Catalogs.* Davis, CA: Passive Solar Institute, 1978–1980.

Daniels, George. *Solar Homes and Sun Heating.* New York: Harper and Row Publishing, 1976.

Gray, Virginia and Alan Macrae. *Mud, Space and Spirit.* Santa Barbara: Capra Press, 1976.

Lumpkin, William. *Casa del Sol.* Santa Fe: Santa Fe Publishing Co.

Mazria, Edward. *The Passive Solar Energy Book.* Emmanaus, PA: Rodale Press, 1979.

Reif, Daniel R. *Solar Retrofit: Adding Solar to Your Home.* Andover, MA: Brick House Publishing, 1981.

Smith, Shane. *The Bountiful Solar Greenhouse.* Santa Fe: John Muir Publishing.

van Dresser, Peter. *Home Grown Sun Dwellings.* Santa Fe: Lightning Tree Publishing, 1977.

Watson, Donald. *Designing and Building a Solar House: Your Place in the Sun.* Charlotte, VT: Garden Way Publishing, 1977.

Watson, Donald and Kenneth Babe. *Climatic Design.* New York: McGraw-Hill Book Company, 1983.

Wright, David. *Natural Solar Architecture: A Passive Primer.* New York: Nostrand Reinhold Company, 1978.

Yanda and Fisher. *The Solar Greenhouse.* Santa Fe.

WHO IS GOING TO BUILD IT?

An executive for a transfer company built his own adobe on week-ends and evenings. A widow in Sandoval designed and built a charming little adobe with the help of local laborers. A secretary laid the floors and helped with construction to cut the cost of her house considerably. I know of two instances where large houses were constructed by teenagers.

You no doubt know someone who has done some or all of his own construction with good results, and the chances are that he is just an ordinary citizen with the usual amount of grey cells but with the ambition to tackle a long, hard job and the ability to keep his eyes open, ask questions, and take advice.

When my husband and I built our first house, we found that people were universally kind and helpful, eager to give us the benefit of their experience. We learned many construction processes simply by watching workmen on the job. Our building supply dealer was a mine of information. Friends suggested someone who might know the answers to the problems we encountered. Some things we learned through the costly process of trial and error. Very few things we have done since have given us the pleasure and satisfaction (and exercise!) that building that little house gave us. Even today we occasionally drive by for a look at it and congratulate ourselves upon finding it still standing. Honesty forces me to admit that if we could do it, almost anyone can.

Before you decide to tackle the actual construction of your adobe, however, better take a self-inventory. Can you saw straight? Drive a nail without mashing a finger? Have you a rudimentary knowledge at least of construction processes? Have you the ability to see things through, or are you a strong starter and a poor finisher? Have you enough capital to finance a good portion of the construction yourself? Lenders are understandably reluctant to advance money to amateur builders. The best you can usually hope for is an arrangement whereby you may borrow the money to finish construction when you have a portion of the work completed.

If you have reason to doubt that you can do a workmanlike job, think twice. The same expensive materials go into a crudely built house as into one which is well built. Poor plumbing and wiring are expensive to repair and replace and can be downright dangerous.

One of the greatest savings of building costs lies in doing some or all of the construction yourself, but being your own builder is not for everyone. If it is not feasible for you and you elect to have a contractor do the building, you may still be able to make a substantial savings simply by spending a little extra time in getting bids on the job. You will find that they may vary to an astonishing degree.

Sometimes a low bid will result when a contractor suggests that you substitute materials less expensive than those you specified but equally satisfactory. If your plan has some design gimmick that is unfamiliar to some, they may bid the job high to protect themselves from loss. Some contractors are more efficient at shopping for materials or less dependent upon a temporary labor force than others and can trim their bids accordingly to win the contract away from competitors. For any or all of these reasons, the bids you receive may have quite a spread. A little shopping may mean dollars ahead.

Up to this point we have assumed that everything has gone smoothly and that the contractors' figure has fallen within the limits of the amount you have decided to spend. Unfortunately, when the bids arrive, the prospective home owner often receives a rude shock. Although he feels that he has cut non-essentials to the bone, the figures submitted seem astronomical. Suppose this happens to you. What to do?

First have the contractors go over the figures carefully with you to be sure that no misunderstanding has arisen as to just what was wanted. Study the breakdown of the costs to see just where all of that money is going to go. Perhaps a sacrifice or two or a substitution will bring the cost within your range.

Could you finish one room or build a garage at a later date? Would a carport instead of a garage be just as satisfactory and somewhat cheaper? How about doing some of the construction yourself. Could you do the leveling and grading, clean brick work, even wash the windows? The contractor will pay someone to do all of these things before the house is turned over to you. Though some of these savings look like pretty small potatoes, keep looking for little economies. They could add up to a respectable amount.

Don't be tempted to skimp on such basics as good plumbing, heating, and wiring, and don't omit features which you consider essential. You may save five hundred dollars by giving up a fireplace, but if a fireplace has always been a feature of your dream house, think first. If you find yourself red penciling too many cherished features, back off and take a long, hard look at the total plan. Better to scrap this one and start over than to settle for an unsatisfactory stripped-down version of the original plan.

It is not always wise to select a contractor merely because he has submitted the lowest bid. Shoddy workmanship, failure to use specified materials, extensive delays or even actual failure to complete the job, mechanics' liens which cloud your title—all can turn your building venture into a nightmare. You must know how to select a contractor and how to protect yourself against these problems.

How? First, select the contractors whom you will contact from those who are established in the community and are of good financial standing. Some you will know by reputation. Others may be recommended by friends with whom they have had satisfactory dealings or by your bank or the lending institution which will finance your new home. Some you may contact after you have seen a house which they have built or are building. These contractors may vary from large organizations to the small builder who does much of the actual construction himself. It is a good idea to go to contractors who specialize in adobe construction if possible.

Contractors often become identified with a particular type of home design. I can think of several local builders whose adobes can be quite readily distinguished because of certain design features that have become almost a trademark. If his houses are well built, do not reject a contractor simply because you do not care for the design of the houses which he habitually constructs, unless you intend to depend upon him for the design of your own. The quality of workmanship which he demands and his ability to get the job done promptly and satisfactorily are what you are shopping for.

Second, be sure that the working drawings and specifications are as explicit and complete as possible and that each contractor thoroughly understands just what you want to be included in the figure he submits.

If you plan to do some of the work yourself, ask the contractor to list an allowance for such work in his bid. The amount of this allowance will be credited to you at the time of your final payment. The work which you intend to do yourself should be inserted in the specifications when a contract is signed and becomes part of the written agreement.

Third, insure a satisfactory completion of the job by signing a contract with the contractor whom you select which specifically outlines his responsibilities, allows you to take over the work if certain conditions are not met, and sets a reasonable time limit for the completion of the job. Have a clear understanding about the procedure to be followed if changes are made after the work has started. Stipulate that a complete release of liens or receipts showing payment in full for all labor and materials must be presented before your final payment will be made, or ask for a waiver of lien.

The contractor may agree to build your house for a certain figure, or he may contract to build it for the cost of the materials plus a percentage (usually ten per cent) for his services. Either arrangement may be perfectly satisfactory. If you agree to a cost-plus arrangement, your liabilities as owner are more extensive than under the first arrangement. Be sure that you understand this. Have a written contract even if the contractor is a personal friend. It prevents misunderstandings and protects you in case of his death or disability before the house is completed.

The following sample contract shows what items are usually covered. Check with your own attorney to be sure that your contract is correctly worded and is as air tight from a legal standpoint as it is possible.

AGREEMENT

This agreement is made and entered into in the City of _____
State of _____ this _____ day of _____
between _____, the purchasers,
and _____ , the contractor.

The contractor shall furnish and pay for all the labor, work, materials, tools, equipment, light, water, power, transportation, and other provisions, including the building site described as follows:

(Legal description)
(If you already own the site, the location and the fact that you own it will be stated.)

which may be necessary to construct, complete, and deliver to the purchaser in good and workmanlike condition, free from all liens or claims, a single family residence and other improvements in accordance with the plans and specifications hereto attached as well as Federal Housing Administration "Minimum Construction Requirements" which shall be considered as a part of the plans and specifications; by a total of 150 consecutive calendar days from the date of this agreement. He shall furnish all surveys, permits, and licenses of a temporary nature needed for the completion of the work.

Any extra work which is done over and above that called for on the plans and specifications attached hereto will be paid for at cost by the purchaser. No changes or alterations shall be made in the work except on written order of the owner which shall be signed by the contractor.

The contractor shall make such corrections in the work and materials as may be necessary to comply substantially with this agreement, either before or after final payment has been made.

The contractor shall comply with all laws and regulations, shall use only new materials unless otherwise specified, shall employ only fit and competent superintendents and employees, shall maintain order on the job, shall protect his work and the interests of the owner and other adjoining and adjacent owners, shall permit and facilitate inspection of the work by the purchaser to insure compliance with this agreement, shall see to it that any taxes incident to the performance of this agreement including taxes for the protection, benefit, or social security of employees of the contractor and any subcontractor are paid and discharged, shall settle and discharge all liens arising out of this agreement, shall be responsible for the work and payment of any subcontractors, shall keep and leave the premises in good and presentable condition, shall furnish the purchaser on request proof of adequate compliance with any of the foregoing requirements satisfactory to this agreement.

The contractor shall at his own cost and expense procure and maintain workmen's compensation and full public liability insurance to cover the liability of the owner and contractor for personal injury, death, property damage, and workmen's compensation arising out of this agreement and shall settle and discharge any claims of liability thereof.

The contractor shall procure and maintain insurance against loss or damage by fire.

The purchaser shall pay the contractor for the performance of this contract, subject to additions and deductions as provided herein, the sum of _____ _____ as follows: (down payment, allowances for work done by owner, and balance)

to be paid upon satisfactory completion of the contract and the presentation by the contractor. of a properly executed Waiver of Lien showing all labor and materials used in erection of the premises as having been paid in full to the purchaser.

IN WITNESS WHEREOF, the parties hereto have hereunto set their hands on the day and year first above written.

(Signatures)

Fourth, you can do a great deal to speed the completion of the work by the way in which you and the contractor can work together. One of the chief causes of misunderstandings lies in making changes once construction has begun. This covers substitutions by the contractor for materials which have been called for in the specifications and changes which are requested by the owner during construction.

Although minor changes can be made with little expense, what seems to be very minor to you may involve a whole chain reaction of changes or greatly slow down the construction schedule and result in a big bill. Be sure you understand and have in writing what each change is going to cost before you authorize the contractor to make it, or you may be faced with some husky additional charges at the time of settlement that you did not anticipate and cannot afford.

Do not ask workmen to make changes without the authorization of the contractor. Many owners make themselves unwelcome on the job by interfering with the normal progress of the work. Some contractors go so far as to banish owners from the site during working hours and heartily wish them in Timbuktu until the house is completed. The relationship between the contractor and the owner calls for forebearance on both sides.

You may also cause unnecessary delays if you are slow to reach decisions about selections of flooring materials, light fixtures, and paint colors. If you are doing some of the labor, such as painting, be sure that you complete the work as promptly as possible. A good contractor makes much of his profit by his ability to handle subcontractors so that each comes in and does his work on schedule. Construction progresses smoothly from one step to the next, and subcontractors do not interfere with or delay each other.

This is one of the most important functions of the contractor. He finances construction, secures the necessary permits, arranges for subcontractors, supervises building, hires and fires some labor, and carries adequate insurance for his protection and yours if someone should be injured on the building site. He arranges for insurance protection for the unfinished structure. He must call for the necessary inspections while the building progresses and secure a final inspection when it is completed.

Contractors sometimes furnish design services as well. This may be no more than allowing you to specify some changes in a standard plan. A few do extensive custom designing. I know of one contractor with training in both art and architecture who designs beautiful custom adobes for a selected few clients, lavishing attention on the smallest detail and often planning some of the furnishings and landscaping as well. These are good houses, good to live in, good to look at. Adobe has been used honestly but imaginatively.

Whether your contractor is a business man or an artist, he may save you a portion of the cost of his services by saving you from making expensive mistakes in design or construction.

Subcontractors are specialists in some aspect of construction; wiring, plumbing, flooring, roofing, and the like. They submit bids on that one phase of construction. If you elect to act as your own contractor and engage the services of various subcontractors, you enter upon separate contracts with each one and pay each one upon the completion of his portion of the work. If subcontractors are engaged by a prime contractor, he sees that they are paid. If he should fail to do so or if you should withhold payment for some reason, the subcontractor (or anyone else furnishing materials and services for the construction of your house) may file a mechanics' lien, a legal claim for payment, against this property. The recording of this claim clouds the title to your property. In order to clear title so that it is marketable, the lien must be paid. If the contractor fails to do so, even though you may have already paid him, you may be forced to pay the lien yourself. There may be more than one lien placed against the property. The first to be recorded has first priority.

A lien may be filed within ninety days after the completion of the work. It may be filed even though the owner has withheld payment to force adjustment of work which he feels has been done unsatisfactorily. Remember that if the work has passed the building inspections and conforms to the specifications, the subcontractor and/or the prime contractor have fulfilled the conditions of their contracts and should be paid.

The best assurance of a good job is the selection of reliable contractors. Prime contractors often employ the subcontractor on job after job. They not only know the quality of the work they are contracting for but also have a lever to force the remedy of any defective work because the subcontractor cannot expect future jobs from them unless performance is satisfactory.

One last word on the problems you may encounter as your house is built. This concerns your liability for injury to the person or property of others while your house is under construction. If you elect to do the building yourself or to subcontract it yourself, you must carry adequate liability insurance protection. Even though you exercise all due caution, post warning signs, and notify neighboring property holders of your intention to build upon the site, you are still considered liable should an accident occur or neighboring property be damaged.

If you have a prime contractor, although you have a contract with him stating that you are not liable for such occurrences, you should have owner's liability insurance. If the contractor is not able financially to meet the claim for damages, suit may well be filed against you.

If you should move into the house before the contractor has completed his work, you should be aware that in this event the contractor's liability has ceased. By your act, you have accepted his work even though the final payment has not been made, and the legal liability passes to you.

Once you have taken possession, however, your contractor is not released from his obligation to see the work through to a satisfactory completion or from the obligation to remedy any flaws in materials and workmanship which appear after the final payment has been made.

Who will build your house? Will you have the excitement of seeing it take shape under your own hands? Will you shop diligently for the services of a contractor? Before you can get on with the actual construction, you will have to have the answer to one other question, Where are you going to get all that money?

WHERE ARE YOU GOING
TO GET ALL THAT MONEY?

Many people borrowing for their first home say that they feel reluctant to approach a lender because they feel as if they are begging for money. Lending money is a business like any other, and you owe it to yourself to shop for money just as you shop for other goods and services to get the type of mortgage and rate of interest which will be most advantageous to you.

There is no magic formula for this. Each home loan transaction involves a unique combination of factors: the type and size of home that is constructed, the building site, the builder, the financial status of the borrower, the type of mortgage desired, and the current conditions in the money market which will influence the rate of interest which must be paid and the ease with which a loan can be secured.

The only way you can find out how much money you can borrow is to go to a lender and ask.

If you build in or near a fairly large community, there will be a number of lenders in competition for the mortgage business. In a small community the local bank could be the only source of mortgage money. Competition among lenders works to your advantage in securing good terms, while competition among borrowers for the funds of one or two lenders will lessen your bargaining position and allow lenders to pursue a very conservative lending policy. Competition among lenders increases when the amount of money available for new construction is plentiful. When interest rates on home loans are low, lenders invest elsewhere for a greater yield, and the money available for new construction decreases.

Who makes mortgage loans besides banks? Savings and loan associations specialize in home financing. Life insurance companies invest heavily in the mortgage market, either by making direct loans or by purchasing mortgages held by other lenders. In 1964, for example, the Prudential Life Insurance Company invested over three million dollars in residential and farm loans in the Albuquerque, New Mexico, area. Some life insurance companies offer loans at a very favorable rate of interest in a package deal with life insurance policies. Mortgage companies lend money on the security of improved real estate. Generally such companies act as agents in obtaining loans from other lenders such as insurance companies. They may also be formed by tract builders to make loans on houses which the company builds and then to discount them as soon as possible to banks and insurance companies. Private individuals also lend money on real estate, especially on short term loans and on property for which other financing is difficult to obtain usually at a high rate of interest.

The real estate broker who assisted you with the purchase of your building site can give you information about what lenders are making loans in that area. Your contractor can give you advice about the current loan situation and what lenders to contact. Discuss your plans with your own bank. Contact your regional FHA office for information about FHA loans. You can learn about the local mortgage situation from them all.

If you have been wise, you have investigated loan possibilities at the time you selected your building site, especially if you plan to build in a rural area where it is sometimes difficult to get financing. For example, in one community it is hard to find lenders interested in mortgages on homes in nearby mountain areas, and interest rates on those which can be obtained are higher than rates within the city to compensate for the greater risk the lenders assume. However, there is considerable competition among lenders for mortgages in certain desirable rural areas in the nearby valley. Generous loans can be had readily and at a very favorable interest rate.

Perhaps at first glance there does not seem to be much difference in an interest rate of 5½% and one of 6%. Before you are tempted to dismiss a difference of one half a percent as unimportant, do a little arithmetic to see just how much it will cost you over the life of a twenty-five year mortgage.

At times a portion of the interest rate quoted may represent loan insurance which guarantees repayment to the lender. Those making

FHA loans are insured against loss by the Federal Housing Administration, which charges the borrower an insurance premium of one half of a percent per year on the average scheduled mortgage loan balance. These payments are included in your monthly payment and are paid into the Mutual Mortgage Insurance Fund by the FHA. It may be to your advantage to know that in some cases home owners may receive dividends from this fund when their mortgages have been paid.

Conventional loans may now be obtained with loan insurance protecting the lender against loss. The advantage of these insured loans is the low down payment which is required. A low down payment and monthly payments spread out over a long period of time may seem very attractive. However, do remember as you arrange the terms of your loan that you will save a sizable sum in your total interest payments if you borrow as little as you can and repay it as quickly as you can. The Federal Housing Administration points out in a booklet on home financing that if you borrow $10,000 at 5¼% for thirty years it will cost you 60% more in total interest than if you had borrowed it for twenty years.

It is not wise to set up a mortgage arrangement which commits most of your reserves for a large down payment thinking you could always refinance your home if necessary. Refinancing is costly, takes time, and may have to be done at a higher interest rate than your present loan.

Shop for a mortgage tailored to your future plans and to possible emergencies as well as to your current needs.

Perhaps you can get an open end mortgage which will allow you to borrow additional advances from the lender at a later date up to the original amount of the loan to make additions or major repairs to your property without the cost of refinancing. Such improvements would otherwise be paid for through separate short term loans with large monthly payments.

A package mortgage includes the cost of major appliances installed in your new home, such as a dish washer or built-in range. You have one long-term loan and one monthly payment. The disadvantage to such an arrangement is the fact that one pays interest over the long term of the home loan for the cost of appliances which will need to be replaced within a relatively short time.

Some loans carry a penalty for prepayment or restrict the manner in which extra payments may be made. If you hope to pay off your mortgage before its full term, be sure you will have a prepayment privilege.

Mortgages are called term or amortizing, depending upon the manner in which they are to be repaid. Term mortgages provide for the semi-annual or quarterly payment of interest but no payment of the principal (the actual amount borrowed) until the end of the mortgage period, which is usually three to five years. At the end of this period, the mortgage can be renewed for another term. During a period of financial panic, renewal of such a mortgage may be difficult or even impossible. Term mortgages were generally in use until the 1930's when the Federal Housing Administration was created by Congress.

The FHA mortgages were set up as amortizing mortgages. Today almost all mortgages are amortizing mortgages, mortgages which provide for a reduction of the principal with each payment. You make monthly payments like rent, and at the end of the mortgage period all the money which you had borrowed plus the interest charges for the use of the money will have been paid.

There are various ways in which these monthly payments can be set up. They may be a fixed figure over the life of the mortgage or may be arranged to decrease or increase during the mortgage period, allowing you to coordinate the size of the payments with your anticipated income.

Once you have found what financing will be available and have selected a lender, you will make a formal mortgage loan application. You will be asked for full details concerning the house you plan to construct, including the plans and the specifications. You will make a statement of your financial affairs: what you earn, what you owe, and what assets you have.

If you apply for an FHA mortgage, the lender will submit an application to the FHA regional office. If your house meets certain minimum standards of construction, the FHA will issue a commitment of insurance, an agreement to insure the repayment of a loan of an amount based upon their appraisal of your house. FHA will also conduct periodic inspections during its construction. The Federal Housing Administration does *not* make home loans. It merely insures the loan's repayment to the lender.

If both your plans and your credit meet with approval, the lender will agree to make the loan by issuing a commitment, a promise to loan a certain amount on your completed house. Usually the money to carry on actual construction must be borrowed in a separate short-term loan. If you have a contractor, he may furnish the construction money when you have made a reasonable down payment to him.

As I have pointed out, those building their own homes may find it difficult or impossible to borrow construction funds, at least until a portion of the house has been satisfactorily completed. Do not begin to build your adobe hoping that you can find someone to finance its completion when your funds are exhausted. Make sure you will be able to get the money to finish it and have a firm commitment on a mortgage figure.

The mortgage will be executed when your house is completed. You will sign a note as mortgagor pledging the house as security for the loan made by the lender, the mortgagee. There will be application fee and credit report charges and other closing costs. You should know in advance just what these charges are to be.

The interest you will pay for the use of the mortgage money is only one of the expenses of home ownership. You must forgo the income you would receive from the equity you have invested in your house. There will be maintenance costs, taxes and other assessments, fire insurance and liability insurance, utilities, and the depreciation of your property through obsolescence and through use.

On the credit side of the ledger, you will be able to charge interest and tax payments off on your income tax. If the present inflationary trend continues, losses from depreciation will be lessened. It will also be easier to repay the fixed number of dollars which were borrowed as dollars become less valuable. Those monthly payments represent a form of savings as your equity in the property grows. There is also the less tangible dividend of family stability and day to day pleasure in living in a good house planned for your family's needs.

If you have done your planning well from the selection of the site to the arrangements for the mortgage, owning your own adobe can be a source of great pleasure and satisfaction.

HOW CAN YOU DO IT YOURSELF?

The building of an adobe house is a process suited to the land of *mañana*. One must have patience for the tedious repetition of molding the bricks. Their curing cannot be hurried, for adobes improve with age. Even after the walls begin to go up, the work must be done with deliberation. Adobe mortar sets slowly, and the walls cannot be carried too high in any one day. Any attempt to hurry the work by using lime mortar seems to result in less structural strength. Adobe bricks and adobe mortar have the same coefficient of expansion, and they tend to blend into a single mass as the mortar sets.

You move slowly round and round the walls. When they are at last high enough for the lintels to be put over the doors and windows, all work must cease for at least a week to allow the mortar to dry more. The lintels must be set three quarters of an inch to an inch higher than the door and window frames to allow for more settling, and the exterior trim should only be tacked in place for a time.

You cannot hurry the plastering, for the walls should cure about six months before Portland cement stucco is applied to them. It is better to use a protective coat of mud plaster for the first year or so before proceeding to stucco.

The deliberate pace of adobe construction seems made to order for the weekend builder.

To the casual observer, putting up an adobe may seem a bit like making mud pies, but there is nothing haphazard or sloppy about a good job. As it is with any other material, good workmanship is necessary if the house is to be structurally sound. To be your own builder you will need a reasonable amount of skill as well as a lot of patience.

You also need TIME. You cannot live too far from your building site, or too much of that precious stuff will be used up in simply getting back and forth to the job. You will have to give up many a week-end fishing trip or a picnic in the mountains before the house is at last completed, and there will be many times when you will be sick of the whole never-ending business.

You must be a good organizer. You must plan ahead to order materials well in advance of their need, to get extra labor or subcontractors on the job when you are ready for them, and to see that necessary inspections are made on schedule so that the work will not be held up. It helps to set up a construction schedule. The construction of an adobe house with on-grade floors would proceed about like this:

> Secure building permit and site inspection if required
> Make or buy adobes and store on site
> Stake out house
> Prepare footings
> Rough in plumbing (inspection if required)
> Rough in heating (inspection if required)
> Lay up adobes, installing window and door frames
> Build fireplaces
> Install interior partitions if not adobe
> Rough in wiring (inspection if necessary)
> Pour bond course
> Roof and put in exterior doors and windows
> Pour concrete floors or install bricks in sand
> Plaster
> Install cabinets and interior doors
> Paint
> Install plumbing fixtures and light fixtures

Do-it-yourselfers may cut construction costs materially by making their own adobes, especially if suitable soil exists on the building site. You can mix adobes with a hoe, a cement mixer, a pug mill, or with your bare feet, as one enthusiastic weekend builder did. You can add straw or horse manure or use a plain mud mix. You may make your bricks any of a number of sizes. There is no one way to make adobes, as talks with several "old-timers" will soon reveal. Good adobes are produced by several methods if one adds a generous dash of experience to the mix.

It takes experience to get the right consistency. Mud too wet will slump. Mud too dry will not mold satisfactorily. It takes experience to tell when a soil will have the right proportions of sand and clay to make a good brick. Not even a soil analysis will guarantee good results. If you have no one with experience to tell by sight and feel that a soil is right or if you cannot use a soil which has already made satisfactory adobes, trial and error will be the only means by which you can arrive at the proper mix. For the novice, a session with test bricks is necessary.

What sort of soil are you to test? The type which is commonly called "adobe" is a heavy clay soil which is hard to mix when wet and which dries with too many shrinkage cracks to make good bricks. A sandy soil produces bricks which crumble too readily. You want a sandy clay or a clay loam. A good soil will barely slip off the hoe as you work the mud and will leave traces of mud on the hoe. Too much clay will make the mud stick to the hoe. Too much sand is indicated if the hoe comes up clean.

Sometimes you can modify a soil to make satisfactory bricks. The old-timers may modify a clay soil by adding sand, straw, or manure to prevent shrinkage cracks. Manure seems to be harmful to the strength of the brick and its durability. Straw will weaken bricks if too much is used. It is useful chiefly as a binder to hold the brick together as it dries. If straw is added, it should be in very short lengths, a good handful per brick. It will take a little more than a one hundred pound bale of straw for a thousand average bricks. Sand can be added to the clay. The proper amount can be determined fairly well by the hoe test. Keep a record of the proportions of sand and clay in each test brick. The soils you test should be reasonably close to your building site and readily available in sufficient quantity to make all the bricks you need.

To shape your test adobes you will need a simple wooden or sheet metal form shaped like a shallow, bottomless box. The inside measurements should be slightly larger than you want the finished brick to be. This allows for shrinkage. A 4x10x14 inch brick is a workable size weighing some thirty pounds. Anything larger is somewhat difficult to handle. Hand holes or handles and a slight inward taper to the form will make it easier to lift it from the molded brick.

Mix the test soil with water in a wheelbarrow, mortar box, or a shallow pit dug in the ground. Moisture must penetrate the entire mass, so mix it well. If you can soak it overnight so much the better, for the water penetrates and softens all the lumps. Add enough water to make a mixture which is stiff enough to be handled with a fork yet workable enough to be tamped into the corners of the mold without clinging to the sides when the form is lifted. You add straw if you desire it after the mud is mixed, scattering it over the surface and working it in.

Mold the bricks on straw or wet sand so that they will not stick to the ground. Fill the dampened form, tamp the mud, strike off the excess mud with a short board, sprinkle the top of the brick with water, and smooth it with your hand. Lift the form from the molded brick. Clean and dampen the form before using it again. Make several bricks of each soil sample.

In a few days the bricks can be handled. Stand them on edge and continue drying them. They should cure about two weeks. Their durability can be tested by exposing them to the weather or by wetting and drying them several times to be sure they will not break down or crumble.

If a test brick cracks excessively, too much clay is indicated. However, poor mixing or too stiff a mix or too rapid drying will also cause cracking, so use care in preparing the mix and shade the bricks for a few days in hot, windy weather to rule out these possibilities. If the test bricks are unsatisfactory, you might modify your soil and make additional samples.

A good adobe brick will not show excessive cracks from drying, will resist abrasion and breakage. It should break only if struck a good blow with a hammer. There are no voids from improper tamping. It should not crumble when wet down.

When your test bricks appear to be satisfactory, you are ready to produce them in quantity using the same equipment and method. These tips may help. Have the soil delivered by dump truck if you cannot use soil on the site, and mix the bricks near the building site for ease in handling the finished bricks. Have an ample supply of water available. Soak enough soil for each day's production overnight to make mixing easier. Mix with a power mixer or by hand in a mortar box or in a large pit (six to eight feet in diameter and two to three feet deep). Use a wheelbarrow to move the mud to the molding area. Dampening it keeps the mud from sticking. The forms may be large enough to mold several bricks at once but not too large for one man to handle easily. Two forms are handy, as one soaks while the other is in use. If a brick begins to crack, you may sometimes salvage two good half bricks by scoring it down the middle.

Allow the bricks to dry several days before attempting to stand them on end. Clean off any irregularities and the loose dirt and straw. When the bricks are thoroughly cured, you can stack them loosely on end and cover them with boards and straw or plastic sheeting. Cure the bricks at least a month before laying them up.

You can estimate how many bricks you will have to make. Figure the area of the outside walls and subtract the area of the door and window openings. Divide this figure by the area (in feet) of the exposed side of the brick. Subtract ten percent.

Waterproof adobe bricks may be made with soil and an asphalt or Portland cement stabilizer in the same manner as regular adobe bricks are made. The presence of alkali salts or too great a percentage of fine particles make a soil unsuitable for use with asphalt. Soils should be tested according to directions furnished by the manufacturers of the stabilizer to be added. The proportions of the mix must be more accurate than those for regular adobes. The higher cost of these bricks can be somewhat offset if they are used without a protective coat of plaster. Though they are not for purists or traditionalists, they lend themselves especially to handsome contemporary treatments.

While the adobes are curing, you can dig the trenches for the footings. Although some old adobe houses are still standing on skimpy foundations of rock and mud mortar or even upon no foundation at all, countless others must have succumbed to the moisture which crept into the walls from the ground and the cracks caused by uneven settling. With so much money, time, and effort to be invested in your adobe, you will want to get things off to a good start by preparing an adequate foundation.

The footings distribute the weight of the house evenly over the soil you build on. Coarse sandy soil can bear more weight than a fine clay soil. For the usual soil conditions, you will need a footing some eight inches wider than your adobe walls and deep enough to go below the frost line so that it will not heave in heavy frosts. It should be of concrete reinforced with steel rods. When you pour the footings, tamp the concrete thoroughly in the dampened forms by moving a shovel up and down in the concrete, especially along the sides of the forms. This will help to prevent honeycomb. Remember that footings are inspected before concrete is poured.

Making adobes on a commercial scale.

Mud mortar may be mixed in a shallow pit like this. Soil should be screened to remove lumps and rocks.

Adobe bricks are laid up without mortar between the vertical joints to provide a bond so that plaster can be secured to the wall.

Adobe under construction. Note wood nailing blocks set into door and window openings. Frames will be nailed to them. The recommended method is to put the frames in place and build the walls around them, anchoring them with metal brick anchors and a 2x2 lug fastened to the frames and set in notches in the adjacent adobes.

Flue linings and metal damper can be used to simplify fireplace construction. Republished courtesy of *New Mexico Magazine*.

Partially completed fireplace with damper and flue liner in place. Note that fireplace is constructed as house walls go up. Republished courtesy *New Mexico Magazine*.

Foundation walls of concrete or masonry as wide as your adobes come next. Any handbook on construction will give clear directions for constructing forms for the footings.

Plumbing and heating rough-ins are ordinarily done before the walls go up. Do-it-yourselfers can buy prefabricated units all made up and ready to put into place. Local plumbing companies can supply these. They can even be ordered by mail order catalog and all the necessary tools can be rented.

If you are building in the country where there is no community sewage disposal system, you will have to construct your own facilities for sewage disposal. The most popular method is the septic tank with an underground leeching system.

If it is well designed, the septic tank will take care of sewage as well as a city sewer. One which is poorly constructed will never function satisfactorily and can become a health menace. County codes require a certain distance from your primary water supply. Check local regulations.

It is customary to locate the septic tank fifteen to twenty feet from the house. Do not place it where it can be damaged by the weight of a heavy truck such as the one which services your butane tank.

You can purchase a metal prefabricated septic tank or construct one of masonry. It must be large enough to serve the number of people who will occupy your house. Figure a capacity of about one hundred gallons per person. If the tank is too small or is improperly cleaned, it may overflow to the ground surface. This results in offensive odors and, worse, a possible spread of disease.

The tank receives your household wastes. Liquids pass out of the tank into a leeching field through tiles. In sandy soils this percolation is too fast to permit oxidation. In heavy clay soils the air is excluded and anaerobic bacteria which cause foul odors can multiply. Heavy clay soils require a larger leeching field. Another solution to this problem is to supply air to the leeching held by the addition of pumice to the soil. Instead of pipes and ditches, you dig a field fifteen to eighteen inches deep and refill it with a mixture of pumice and soil. This mix will vary from thirty to sixty percent depending upon the soil. You lay drain tiles in this mixture just below the surface. Aerobic bacteria can function and sewage disposal is efficient. There is a lateral as well as a downward movement of water. What you aim for in the leeching field is the even distribution of the waste and its effective oxidation.

A deposit of solids will remain in the septic tank. There are no chemicals which you can add to reduce them, and they are going to require a periodic cleaning. This is not a job for the home handyman. The residue is odorous and often disease carrying and should be disposed of by professionals who make it a business to clean the tanks properly and remove the residue safely.

A tank will need cleaning about once every two years, depending upon the size of the tank and the amount of sewage handled daily. If you plan to have a garbage disposer and flush ground-up garbage down the sink, the solids will build up more quickly. You should make a yearly inspection. When the total depth of scum and solids is more than one third of the depth of the liquid in the tank, a cleaning is indicated.

Failure to have the tank cleaned allows solids to clog the tiles in the leeching field. The whole system may have to be relocated. Tree roots also clog tiles. Keep this in mind as you locate the tank and as you plan your landscaping.

When the rough-ins are completed, you are at last ready to lay the by now thoroughly cured adobes. You can make a mud mortar from the same soil you used for making your bricks. (Screen it, please, and no straw this time.) Mix it with a hoe in a mortar box or in a shallow pit. Add enough water to make mortar which will squeeze out under the bricks as you lay them without tamping them.

Old-timers will probably lay the adobes without mortar in the vertical joints between the bricks. They learned to do this so that their mud plaster would have a bond to secure it to the wall, the same function as that of the chicken wire which is nailed over the wall to hold the stucco. Some builders slush the joints full of mortar.

Adobe bricks may be laid up so that their longest dimension is the width of the wall, or a course laid up in this manner may be alternated with a course in which the bricks are laid with the narrow dimension side by side. For example, 4x8x16″ bricks laid up like this would make a wall 16 inches thick.

To build up a thicker wall, two walls may be laid up with an air space between them. Insulation such as sawdust or pumice could fill the space. Some buildings designed by Santa Fe architect William Lumpkins have adobe walls 24 inches thick built up of ten inch wide bricks with a four inch space between them. The outside wall is gradually sloped inward until the bricks meet and meld producing a gentle upward curve called batter which is very pleasing to the eye. The curve is continued in the parapet which extends above the roof.

The course should be laid up with one-half to three-quarter-inch joints. Build them up in uniform stages. You cannot build up the corners several feet higher as brick masons sometimes do or the walls will settle unevenly. Like fired bricks, adobes are laid up with bonded corners. No bricks should lap less than six inches. A vertical joint never comes over a joint in the course below it. Begin laying the bricks at the corners. Use a taut chalk line as a guide as the brick masons do. You should set the corner bricks so that their top surfaces are all the same distance above the foundation. This will keep the courses level all around the house. Lay up any inside partitions which are built of adobe at the same time.

It is probably better to set your door and window frames in as the walls go up, anchoring them with metal masonry anchors, than to put in wooden nailing blocks to which the frames may be nailed later. Nail a 2x2 wooden strip up the sides of the frames. This will fit into notches cut in the bricks which are to be laid up against the frame. You could cast adobes with this notch, but it is more satisfactory to cut it while the adobes are still green. You use a shaped piece of metal like you would a cookie cutter to cut out a piece of the required size.

As your walls get higher, you may need to shore up a long wall with timbers temporarily so that it won't blow down.

Call a halt when the walls reach the tops of the door frames and let the mud mortar dry out at least a week before you install the lintels over the door and window openings to carry the weight of the wall above them. Use a lintel long enough to lap over a foot on each side, or pour a continuous bond course of reinforced concrete along the top of the wall.

Fireplaces go in before the roof goes on. You must put in concrete footings to support the weight of the fireplace walls and chimney.

Use fire brick for the fire box and use flue liner. Although adobe is fireproof, heat will cause the mud mortar to crumble. Amateur builders would do well to use a prefabricated metal damper for corner fireplaces.

Metal fireplace forms take the guesswork out of fireplace construction for fireplaces built along the wall. You can buy units which come complete with lock-on chimney sections. You place the form on a prepared firebrick hearth, build up around the three sides with concrete masonry block, install the chimney by twist-locking its sections together, and fill the space between the masonry block and the form with mortar and rubble. Your fireplace is then complete except for facing it and building an adobe chimney housing above the roof. The facing can be anything you design, traditional or contemporary as you desire. These fireplace forms come in so many sizes that you can buy one with almost any size of fireplace opening. Not only do they save time in installation, but they are sure to draw. This is not to imply that a satisfactory masonry fireplace cannot be constructed by the amateur builder. After all, most of the oldtimers who built adobes (and adobe fireplaces) were do-it-yourselfers.

Diagrams and charts which will help you design the throat, shelf, and smoke chamber correctly are as close as the nearest library or building supply dealer. It is important to carry the chimney high enough above the house roof (at least two feet) if it is to draw well. Sometimes tall trees close to chimneys will affect the way a fireplace draws. As a rough rule of thumb, the area of the flue lining opening should be one tenth the size of the area of the fireplace opening.

The tiny, rounded corner fireplace of adobe has a special appeal for most adobe enthusiasts, but other types of fireplaces which were built in early adobes are equally charming. The fireplace sometimes had a long hood in the form of a mud shelf, high as a man's head and supported by short lengths of *latias*. The fire was built in the corner on a low raised hearth. Often a *banco* ran along the wall under the hood, a cozy place to sit and toast by the fire. I could not help but think as I looked at a fireplace like this in a recent display at the Folk Art Museum in Santa Fe how attractive it would look in the family kitchen of a present day adobe.

Some very nice fireplaces just happen. There is a corner fireplace in Placitas with a little niche on one side of the chimney, quite high, which looks as if it had been made especially for the Santo displayed there, although it resulted when the builder corrected the slant of a chimney which was getting out of line. However, it ordinarily takes care to design one with pleasing proportions. Since a fireplace becomes the focal point of the room, it is as important that it be pleasing to look at as that it draws well.

Drawings showing the design and construction details of your fireplace will probably be required when you apply for a city building permit, and your fireplace construction will be inspected.

When the fireplace is completed and the ceiling joists have been installed, you are ready to roof the house. A 2x8 bolted to the adobe bricks serves as a bearing plate to distribute the load of the roof evenly along the walls of the house.

A flat built-up roof is commonly used with adobes. Do-it-yourselfers may experience trouble in installing a flat roof which won't leak. If an earth roof is installed it should be carefully compacted and graded so that it will drain. Insulation is installed before hot tar roofing is in place. Fiberglas, sheet board or coarse pumice eight to twelve inches thick, packed and graded, can be used for this. The house walls are built up beyond the roof for several courses to form a parapet. The joint between the roof and the parapet must be flashed and made as water tight as possible. Provide enough roof drains to carry moisture off the roof quickly. A slight slope to the roof aids drainage. The roof parapets are pretty vulnerable to moisture and should be protected with Portland cement stucco. Brick copings, used in the Territorial style, will also protect them.

Another spot where leaks commonly occur is at the point where *vigas* extend through the walls. You should caulk carefully around the *vigas*. Shape the top of the *vigas* to a slight slant so that water will run away from the walls. Moisture dripping from the end of the *vigas* may run along the under side back toward the walls.

Pitched roofs with an overhang give the best protection for adobe walls and fewer opportunities for leaks. In northern New Mexico, where the annual precipitation is much more than in most of the state, many adobes have steep pitched roofs of corrugated galvanized steel to shed snow and rainfall quickly. The material is long lasting, relatively cheap, and easily handled. Corrugated steel roofs require a pitch of at least 3 in 12 but many are steeper with windows in the gable ends or small doors reached by outside stairways.

It is important to have windows in opposite ends of the gabled roof so that airflow can exhaust the heat radiated by the metal roof in summer. Insulation over the house rafters, shiny side up, will reflect the heat back. In winter the underside of the metal roof tends to reradiate heat escaping from the house through the ceiling, thus holding heat in.

Corner fireplace warms the kitchen of the Benc-sics home, Sandoval.

Small corner fireplace. Los Torrones Apartments, Albuquerque.

Fireplace in Gale study was built against a short wing wall. Low adobe wall at left separates the study from a spacious entry landing and a sunken livingroom. Nat Kaplan, designer.

Corner fireplace, Eastman home.

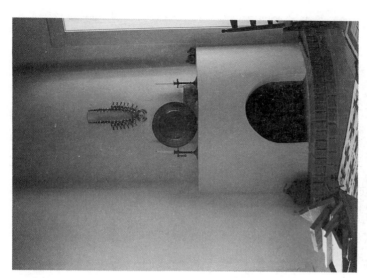

White washed fireplace makes excellent foil for fine Indian necklace and antique accessories. Miller home.

Two shallow tiers provide space for the display of interesting accessories. Witherspoon home.

The corner fireplace moves out on the porch at Krogdahl home.

Traditional corner fireplace gets a contemporary flavor. Hap Crawford, designer.

Small eye-level fireplace in a bedroom wall at the A. Knight residence.

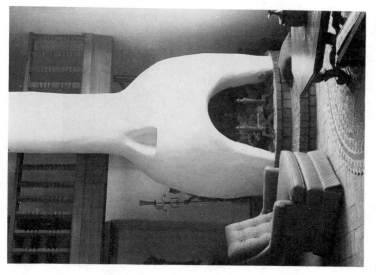

Dramatic free standing fireplace designed by Hap Crawford.

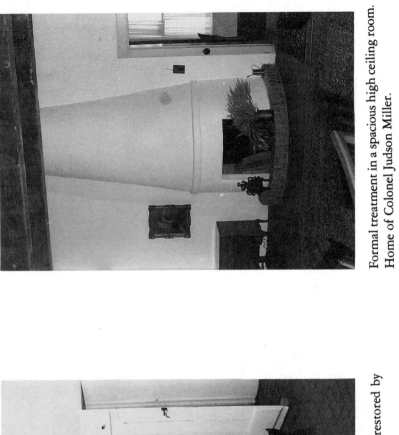

Formal treatment in a spacious high ceiling room. Home of Colonel Judson Miller.

An original fireplace of the adobe restored by Lienaus in Sandoval.

Tiny study fireplace is Indian-built and features an interesting cupboard above. Houle home, Espanola.

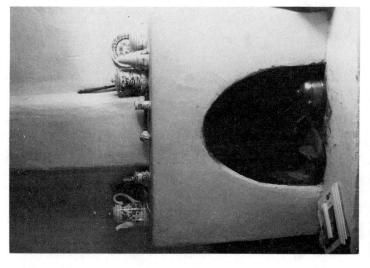

Kitchen fireplace, Krogdahl home.

Handsome kitchen fireplace is built back to back with living room fireplace. Artist-owner achieved a handsome sculptured effect very pleasing to the eye. Richard Sandoval home, Espanola.

Wingwall divides entry from bedroom hallway. Rugs and serapes hang across doorways and slide on rod. They add color and do not take up floor space as a door would. Tiny Indian-built fireplace welcomes guests. Home of Faith Wait, Pojoaque.

Corner fireplace with stone mantel was constructed like early Indian fireplaces, without a smoke shelf. It draws well when fire is laid tepee fashion in back. Home of Mr. and Mrs. Jan Cummings, Albuquerque.

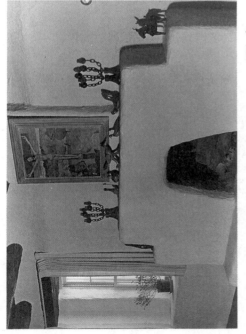

Family room fireplace, Ault adobe, Cedar Crest. Window recess has interesting treatment, indicates depth of outside walls.

Kitchen fireplace, Ault adobe, Cedar Crest, was constructed by Mrs. Ault from a sketch in a *New Mexico Magazine* showing a cross section of a typical corner fireplace.

Note the effective use of Mexican tile on the hearth of this large corner fireplace.

A pitched roof may be framed on the job or may be constructed of roof trusses already assembled and trucked to the site.

With the roof on, interior finishing can begin. Stabilized bricks need not be plastered. Before they are painted, however, they should be given a prime coat of white Portland cement and water (one bag of cement to six gallons of water). Keep the walls damp for several days until the wash has set. Then apply oil paint as usual. Dry wall texture can be used as a finish and is applied after water brushing the walls.

Regular adobes can be given a coat of mud plaster and painted or white washed. Unfinished mud plaster rubs off on clothing. A painted dado which would end this condition would be an attractive wall treatment.

It is not necessary to use wire mesh to bond mud plaster to the wall, but don't forget that mud plaster will not adhere to any partitions that are not adobe. You can probably use the soil you used for adobes to make your plaster. Screen it through fine mesh. Mix a small sample with water to form a thick paste and try it on a dampened wall. If it cracks or comes away from the wall, try again. Use a trowel or your hands. Air is sometimes trapped in pockets in the adobe wall when a trowel is used. When a sample adheres satisfactorily, you can plaster the wall. Prime the plaster when dry with boiled linseed oil and you can paint it with an oil base paint.

You can put commercial plaster directly on adobe walls but you should use mesh at the corners and around the doors and windows. Many builders use mesh all over the walls. It may be required by your lender. Make a depression in the adobe by a blow from the head of your hammer and drive a ten-penny, zinc-coated nail in at an angle to nail on mesh. Dampen the walls before applying the plaster.

When the plastering is completed, you can install the floors. Bricks laid with mortar on cement and brick laid in sand make satisfactory on-grade floors. They are attractive and durable and probably easier for the do-it-yourselfer to install than a concrete slab. Follow the directions given in the following chapter for installing patio flooring. Bricks may be sealed and waxed. Remember that the glossier the finish, the more every footprint will show.

If you want something different in flooring, why not pour yourself a mud floor?

Until the arrival of the Yankee sawmills in the middle of the

1800's, New Mexicans had earthen floors. They swept and sprinkled them to keep the dust down. They sometimes sealed them with animal blood or with a mixture of blood and ashes. They covered them with rugs if they could afford it. And they were very happy to have wooden floors when they were available.

Today in the Taos area and in the vicinity of Santa Cruz one occasionally sees earthen floors of a different sort. A deep burnished brown in color, they appear to be constructed of carefully fitted flagstone, but they are actually made of mud. They are completely durable and satisfactory under ordinary conditions of wear and tear and are extraordinarily attractive. Thin high heels or hobnailed boots might mar them, but floors of this kind have withstood everyday traffic for twenty years protected only by an occasional waxing.

Anyone who has made mud pies can handle the simple though laborious process by which they are constructed. This is the opinion of Miss Augustine Stoll, who had these handsome floors in her Santa Cruz ranch house and more recently in her home at Placitas. The method of construction may vary a little, but this is Miss Stoll's recipe.

Any soil which can be used for making adobe bricks may be used for this floor. Screen the soil to remove lumps and rocks. Mix it thoroughly with water to the same consistency as the mud used to make adobes. "About like fudge," is the way Miss Stoll describes it.

Pour a slab about four inches thick. The area upon which the floor is to be poured must be smooth and level and dampened. All of the floor for one room must be poured in one day if it is to appear uniform and so it will not show a joint where the pouring began again. Level the slab with hand towels and by eye rather than with a screen which may leave marks on the surface.

Allow it to dry approximately ten days. At the end of this period it may be safely walked on. A number of cracks will have developed during drying. These cracks are now filled with adobe slip, mud thin enough to pour from a container with a spout such as a watering can.

After the slip has dried (usually three or four days), paint the floor liberally with boiled linseed oil. In about a week when the floor has cured and is dry again, apply a second coat of boiled linseed oil which has been thinned with one quart of turpentine to the gallon of linseed oil to hasten the drying time. Finish with several thin coats of a good floor wax.

If further cracks develop with time, the floor is easily repaired by filling the crack with slip and treating the area with linseed oil. If a section becomes damaged, you can cut away the damaged area, fill it with mud, and go through the steps outlined above.

Flagstone and terrazzo are other flooring materials that can be used. Brick on sand has one definite advantage over other types of ongrade flooring materials. The bricks can be rather easily taken up and later replaced if it is necessary to make repairs to the plumbing pipes and heating ducts or pipes which are located in the floor.

With the installation of cabinets, counter tops, and ceramic tile, door and window trim, plumbing and light fixtures, and with the attendant small irritations such as trying to find electric outlets which have been covered over in the plastering, only a final painting and touch ups remain to be done.

The clean, bare house awaits the furniture, accessories, memorabilia, and clutter which will give it your personal stamp, and the magic touch of landscaping which will make your home complete.

Since the problems of the construction of adobes with on-grade floors are in general the same as the problems of constructing a concrete masonry house with concrete flooring, any of a number of good manuals on this type of construction will be most helpful. In addition, a list of helpful publications may be secured from the Superintendent of Documents, Government Printing Office, Washington D.C. 20402. County extension agents, the Soil Conservation Service and the USGS are sources for information on soil types in your area. Check your library for the local plumbing and heating codes.

Detail in the kitchen of the Eastman home showing how construction elements become decorative elements when walls are unplastered.

Wall shelves. Gifford home, Corrales.

Earthen floors some forty years old have a soft gloss and a deep brown tone which is restful and attractive. Floors were finished with boiled linseed oil to which a little burnt sienna was added. They have been waxed occasionally over the years. A few settling cracks have been patched with mud. Floors are comfortable to live on. They would not be too durable under extremely hard use. Note the slight undulations in the surface from hand troweling. Home of Mrs. Homer Boss, Santa Cruz.

Old shutters from Mexico installed in Cummings home, Albuquerque. Doors like this would be handsome in a pass-through.

Handsome old wall cupboard. Los Luceros, Alcalde, New Mexico.

Spindles decorate opening between entry hall and living area. Hallway lintel projects through wall to add interest. This corner is interesting even before furnishings and accessories are placed in the room. Nap Kaplan, designer.

Detail of corbel.

Timber carried through adobe wall is made an architectural feature in a house designed and built by Nat Kaplan.

Ceiling in Manier living room is made of peeled poles.

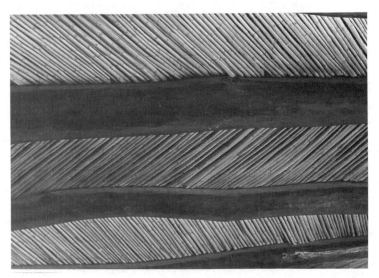

Ceiling in lobby of old Amador Hotel building, Las Cruces, is bamboo. Fine matting can also be used with great effect.

Ceiling in library at Manier home, Corrales. Curves were formed of wire and plastered.

Detail of heavy timbers and woven willow ceilings in the entry hall of the deWerd home, Corrales. Willow ceilings are installed under a double roof, insulation sandwiched between two layers of decking topped with a layer of fifty pound felt, mopped, a layer of twenty five pound felt, mopped, and a layer of twenty five pound felt, mopped and topped with gravel.

HOW DOES YOUR GARDEN GROW?

Landscaping pays off from a strictly dollars and "sense" point of view. Although it will often represent an investment of five to ten percent of the cost of your house and site, it can enhance the value of your property by as much as fifteen percent or more.

Even the most artfully designed house benefits from landscaping. A little nonentity of a house can become a virtual Cinderella. Landscaping performs the sleight-of-hand magic that can make a house seem larger or a bad house more distinctive, give a tract house individuality, correct bad proportions, or screen an undesirable view.

Through good landscaping every high-priced foot of space from lot line to lot line can be utilized and enjoyed by you and your family. Gone is the day of the "front" yard and "back" yard. We no longer landscape just to make the house look attractive from the street, although this is still a valid objective. Today we must accomplish much more than this: no less than the total use of the site.

The micro climate can be modified by the planting of shade trees and vines the selection of planting and paving, the creation of sun pockets, and by wind shelters and overhead baffles to break up wind turbulence. The living areas of the house can be extended visually and actually by outdoor living areas. Service areas containing drying yards, potting sheds, garages, incinerators, and off-the-street parking can be convenient and attractive. The childrens' play yards can be an inviting part of the total design.

These, along with the walls and fences, walks and driveways, are the bones, the framework of the garden. They define its limits and its functions. To complete the plan you must add appropriate plant materials. There may be a hobby garden of iris or roses, if it is a green thumb family. A low maintenance parking strip and a few handsome specimen plants may be all another family desires.

Your landscaping must take into consideration the interests and habits of your family if it is to be successful. Do you like to cook out? Do the children need paving for roller skating and tricycle riding? Is everyone too busy to give more than casual attention to the plants? You must plan for the *people* whom you are going to plant in your garden. And people will add motion, color, and interest to your design.

Your house and its site will also affect the design of your garden. Suppose that your house is small. The use of an oversized tree and shrubs could emphasize its diminutive size and make it look quaint and cozy. To make it appear larger, you would use smaller trees and shrubbery carefully scaled to its size, perhaps a flowering crab tree and a low edging of Santolina along the patio paving. Adobe walls, fences, screens, or strong horizontal lines in the planting will make the house seem wider or longer and increase its apparent size. A wall or planting some distance in the foreground which hides a corner or corners of the house will give the same effect, for the eye does not measure then the size of the house at a glance.

If your lot is small, you might borrow space from your neighbor's plot by tying your landscaping in with his to make both seem larger. If possible use the same plant materials and similar design elements.

In a small space an informal planting may look a bit untidy unless it is carefully planned to get the maximum effect from a few specimens. Plants should be spaced rather than massed, as the latter gives the effect of overcrowding. Use plants with fine to medium foilage textures. Select paving materials like brick which has a fine texture rather than rough, coarse-textured materials like flagstone.

Dark-surfaced fencing tends to recede while light surfaces tend to close in. Try not to stress the boundaries of a small plot or to highlight the corners, as this intensifies the impression of a small enclosure. Break up a long, narrow plot into smaller areas or change levels, because long straight lines leading the eye from front to back will make it seem more narrow. Instead you might lay out your garden on a diagonal axis. Diagonal lines will make it appear to have more width.

For a large plot, plan walks and walls large enough to be in scale. Use rough-textured paving materials and plants with large leaves for

High walled patio close to the house gives privacy to a country house. It is the only formal landscaping device needed. Hap Crawford, designer. Peralta.

Entrance court has a low adobe wall for a sense of enclosure without interfering with a spectacular view of the neighboring mountains. Tappan garden.

Animals are a feature of the informal landscaping of the Krog-dahl adobe.

Twisted pine and rounds of wood were used by Mrs. Owens to lead the eye to the main entrance of her Corrales adobe.

A large chamisa plant against an adobe wall relates the house to its country site and is all the landscaping needed or desired. Chamisa is an attractive, hardy native which can be used throughout the state.

Soapweed and cactus hold shifting sand and make the transition between a small patio garden and the natural landscape. Occasional raking is the only care required now that the planting is established. Rose garden, Corrales.

Tamarisk, soapweed, cactus. These drought resistant natives are used along an adobe wall at the Hopkins home, Corrales.

Chamisa and Russian olive used in a soft informal planting by a garden wall.

Simple vine-covered "shade" makes this spot pleasant for outdoor dining.

Loop drive and a simple planting are used in place of the conventional front lawn. Guests enter the house from an entry garden.

Lathe eyebrow shades a west window.

Wind scoop, a break in the wall surrounding a small patio, invites the prevailing breezes. Gale garden.

Bamboo poles admit breeze but filter sun.

Wood fencing breaks the wind but permits some breeze. Fencing like this can be constructed by the home owner.

Grove of young trees created in the margan. Ludlow garden in Santa Fe.

Grapestake fence. Gravel mulch and difference in leaf textures in the planting add interest. Dark adobe walls or fencing prolong the growing season. Hopkins garden.

Patio wall, Kimmons home, Corrales.

Small wing wall of adobe suggests an entrance court. Wing walls are used for breaking up a long expanse of wall, to form a backdrop for a planting, or to suggest a visual separation of garden elements. Utton garden.

Another view of the garden wall at the Kimmons home, Corrales.

Patio entrance at Krogdahl home suggests a zaguan.

Patio entrance, Rose garden.

Small dooryard garden whose handsome planting is an effective foil for a lovely old door. Edwards garden.

Note the mailbox set into the wall protecting an entry garden in Old Town, Albuquerque.

Small door from an old adobe was installed in the entrance to the patio of the A. Knight garden, Albuquerque.

Simple but inviting gate. Johnson garden.

Saplings were used to construct a low maintenance gate in keeping with a rural setting by Charles Weldman, Corrales.

Stabilized adobes used to reinforce a bank blend with planting and have proven to be durable. Picture was taken several years after installation. Friedman home, Nambe.

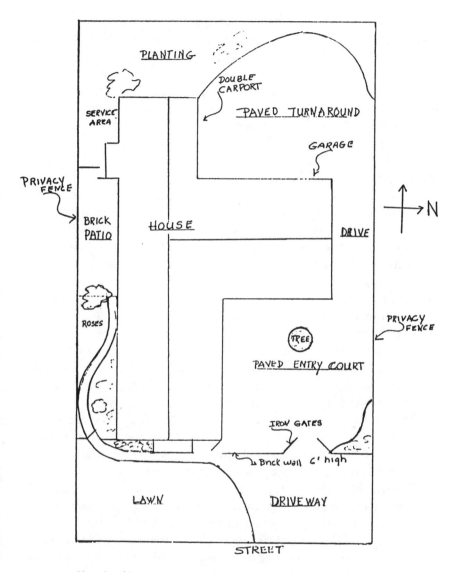

Sketch of house and grounds.

emphasis. Consider using part of the space for off-the-street parking and an area for turning automobiles for the increased comfort and safety of your guests. Don't overlook the possibility of an entrance garden, if the set-back requirement is deep.

Corner lots are often walled for privacy from the street. As an alternative you might plan a high-walled private patio close to the house with perhaps a low maintenance planting for the balance of the plot. Investigate the possibility of a deck to capitalize on a sloping site. Retaining walls and terracing are not the only solution for a plot of this type.

If you live in the country, your landscaping may be confined chiefly to relating the house to the site with a simple native planting, providing for adequate access and parking for several automomiles, and perhaps planting tree belts or hedges to break the force of the prevailing winds. Shelter belts planted at right angles to the direction of the prevailing winds will give some protection as far as twenty times the height of the trees in them, with the most effective protection to areas within eight times their height. They also give some protection close to the windward side.

Remember that corrals and outbuildings, windmills and water towers are all landscaping elements. Animals can also be an interesting part of your landscape design. One of my favorite adobes has as its "view" a pasture in which several fine horses graze.

Take advantage of surrounding vistas. If a pasture fence interrupts the view, perhaps you will want to go to the trouble of constructing a ha-ha, a fence lowered into a ditch which controls livestock but permits an uninterrupted sweep of landscape.

Finally, the orientation of your site with respect to the sun will affect the location and design of the outdoor living areas and the selection of plant materials. While a few shrubs like Mahonia appear to thrive in almost any exposure, most plants require specific growing conditions if they are to flourish, shade for some and full sun for others. These requirements cannot be ignored in your planning.

If you take a drive and look at the landscaping which others have done, you will find that some types of plantings have more appeal to you than others. It is important to know what you like before you begin the final phase of planning. Just what effect do you wish to achieve?

Perhaps you admire the plantings in which rocks, gravel, and twisted pines or pinons are often the dominant elements. They are low maintenance gardens and as such have wide appeal for those who are unable or unwilling to cope with the problems of alkaline soil, drying winds, hot sun both summer and winter, and supplementary watering which plague gardeners in much of the Southwest. Strictly speaking, these gardens are Japanese in inspiration. The Japanese garden is laid out in traditional forms. It is usually small and suggests a natural setting through the sparing and judicious use of carefully chosen natural materials and decorative accessories. Water is often incorporated into the design, dripping from a small fountain, reflecting a bit of sky in a small bowl, or even merely suggested by the placing of rocks and water-worn pebbles to imitate a stream bed. Plant materials are carefully selected for shape, color, and texture; but they are not necessarily the major design element of the garden.

Southwest gardens of this type, especially those making use of native plants, seem quite at home in the New Mexico landscape. They are effective if well designed and suitable for the character of the site. There is no waiting for the grass to grow and for the gaps in the planting to fill in. The garden looks complete on the day it is installed.

It is important to select plants with a slow rate of growth or those which can be kept within bounds easily through occasional pruning and shaping. You must also select plants with similar requirements for water and micro climate, well adapted to local growing conditions, if you expect it to be a low maintenance planting. Do not be deceived by the apparent simplicity of these gardens. It requires skill and meticulous planning to design a good garden of this type.

You may find that an informal sprawling chamisa planting against an adobe wall seems most attractive. A secluded Spanish patio with paving and perhaps a fountain may set you to dreaming of such a spot behind your own adobe walls. Water in the garden adds a note of coolness much appreciated in New Mexico.

Most adobe houses seem to take kindly to a rather informal type of landscaping. Consider the use of drought-resistant native plantings near adobe walls. The soft red-green of the Chamisa and Russian Olive, and the feathery pink plumes of the thoroughly adapted import, Tamarisk, will blend happily with the earth tones of the house. Natives are adapted to the vagaries of the local climate and soil. The use of regional plant materials seems especially appropriate for houses built of a regional material like adobe.

In earlier days, plants were kept away from the house walls of adobe because they were vulnerable to moisture and splashing water. This practice has merit today. Patios, portals, and paving tend to push the plantings away from the house walls where they create an effective frame for the house.

Some gardeners will be drawn to a more formal garden full of flowers and trimmed turf and neatly bordered, carefully mulched rose beds. Perhaps you like the challenge of raising exotic plants which take a great deal of coddling and fussing. If you like to garden, by all means have them. Make your landscaping personal, but do make it suitable in scale and general tone to your house. The garden and house should look as if they belong together!

Once you have your requirements in mind, the actual planning can begin. At this point you may call in a landscape architect, consult a nursery, or accept the challenge and have the fun of planning it yourself. Do as the professionals do and put your plan on paper.

You might properly begin by doodling sketches of various ways in which your garden could be arranged. Do not worry about plants and flower beds at first. Locate the major elements of the design, the driveway, outdoor living area, and service areas. Even a small plot will offer several alternatives, and your solutions should depend upon the needs of the family which will live in your garden.

If you own several automobiles, for example, adequate off-the-street parking and a turning area may be a major part of the landscape design. An ardent gardener will devote much more of the plot to plantings than a home owner who is chiefly interested in developing his site for large-scale outdoor living and entertaining, or one who merely wants things to look neat and attractive with as little trouble as possible.

Don't skimp on the size of the major areas and do anticipate future needs. If you have youngsters growing up, they may need party space or room for a second car. Complete only a portion of the garden at a time if you must, rather than settling for something less than you need and want. Cut corners by the imaginative use of less expensive materials and by doing some of the construction yourself.

Try for simplicity of design. Depend on plant textures and color and the textures of brick, stone, weathered wood, gravel, and paving to provide richness and interest. Use simple forms, the square, rectangle, or, with restraint, the circle. Plan your garden to look well even before grass, trees, flowers, and shrubbery are added. Make it large enough so that when the plants are added they will not overpower or confuse the pattern.

Gardens which have a strong design before the plants are added will look attractive no matter what the season is. They will look "finished" before the planting achieves maturity. Overgrown or straggling plants can be removed and replaced later without upsetting the visual balance. There is less maintenance than there is in gardens depending upon the plant material for form. In the Southwest, growing conditions are trying, and vegetation tends to be sparse in many areas, so it is natural for us to use grass, trees, shrubs, and flowers for the enhancement rather than the structure of the garden. Certainly gardens of this type are in keeping with our Spanish heritage. The Hispanic-Arabic garden with its sheltered patio embellished by paving, fountains, and iron work was strongly architectural in character.

Try to break away from stereotyped solutions. Why must one always locate the patio at the back of the house? If set-back restrictions will permit it, the outdoor living area might better be located at the front behind some screening shrubs, a fence, or an adobe wall. It could be divorced entirely from the house and located at some spot which has an especially lovely view or which would provide a pleasant prospect to be viewed from the house. It could be completely sheltered by the wings of the house or defined by no more than the canopy of a big shade tree or the extent of its paved floor. Instead of one area, there might be several, a small spot by the kitchen door ideal for a leisurely breakfast, a secluded garden off the bathroom for sunbathing, a cool corner in a shady yard furnished by a chair or two.

Why fence the whole yard for privacy if the outside living areas are secluded? Think about mounded earth pushed up to protect a country house from the sight and sound of a busy road. To make walls more interesting you might build them in staggered sections, one behind and overlapping the other. No gate will be needed to fill an access opening.

Place plants where they can be seen from the house rather than using a foundation planting. Foundation plantings are proper for two-storied houses or those with high foundations, but they are really not appropriate for the low one-storied house of the Southwest. They make windows hard to clean and the walls hard to paint. In a few years, unless carefully chosen with an eye to their eventual size, most foundation plantings become overgrown and quite overpowering. The country adobe with its hard-packed earthen dooryard embellished by a graceful tree and a bush rose on a bit of picket fence shows us the charm which minimum plantings can achieve.

The open front lawn may call for some softening planting by the house, perhaps an open, rounded shrub or two, but not a solid overgrown or over-trimmed mass. The walled entry garden frames the house more effectively than a foundation planting and brings the garden out where those in the house can see and enjoy the plants. It is a device that should be used much more often in Southwestern landscaping. A yard too shallow for an entrance garden might well become an off-the-street parking area separated from the street by screen, partial wall, or an island planting.

Did it all sound quite simple to plan a garden until you sat down before a blank sheet of paper? If you are at a loss about beginning, why not start by sketching in the shape of the house and trying to visualize where the outdoor living area might best be located. Keep these requirements in mind:

First, it should be easy and pleasant to move into it from the house. If there are steps they should be broad and inviting. (They will be more comfortable if you remember to use the formula "twice the riser plus the tread should equal twenty-six inches" when you design them.) If there is to be a path leading to the area, it should be broad enough for two people to move on it abreast comfortably. If it is to be used for outdoor cooking, it should be convenient to the kitchen. If you entertain a good deal, it should be readily available from the living room or the family room.

Second, it should be comfortable. Wind turbulence may develop where the wind sweeps over the house roof and swirls downward on the other side. A living area located against the house on the side opposite the direction of the prevailing winds may be unpleasantly breezy much of the time unless a tree deflects the wind or a wind scoop is constructed to deflect the wind back upward as it rolls off the roof edge.

It may be difficult to protect a patio on the west side of the house from the low rays of the late afternoon sun without a screen or a sun-shade of some sort unless existing trees protect it. You might consider erecting a breathing wall such as those used in South America. It is a free standing wall close to the house, so constructed that air can move readily through it but the sun's rays are deflected. It often takes the form of a decorative grill. I have seen a temporary breathing wall constructed of reed screening which shaded the house wall until a planting of trees became large enough to do so.

Even a patio on the north side will need some control of the western sun. Without sun protection a concrete slab will grow uncomfortably warm during the day. The heat radiating from the paving might be welcome warmth in the evening, however, in areas where the temperatures drop quickly after sundown.

Shade from young trees may have to be augmented with a temporary or permanent structure for sun control. One method is to roof the area with solid roofing or with lattice. Woven bamboo blinds or redwood snow fencing can be used for roofing, wired to a steel or wooden frame. A canvas awning is easily installed. Brush can be wired to a rough wooden frame to make a structure like a Navajo "shade."

Vines could be trained on a trellis. Quick growing annuals such as the morning-glory or flowering bean will fill in until a more permanent planting has matured. Wisteria will eventually cover a wide area. It grows very freely and will need a strong support. Silver Lace vine grows rapidly and will flourish in full sun even in poor soil. Grapes could be used on a heavy support. The climbing roses such as Paul's Scarlet, Blaze, or one of the climbing hybrids will grow well. Clematis and honeysuckle prefer shade or partial shade, but honeysuckle will grow in a sunny location, and clematis likes its head in the sun and its roots shaded. Use a mulch for an underplanting. Virginia Creeper can be adapted to a trellis but can be difficult to keep under control and is subject to infestations of small striped worms.

Sun control devices for south patios might well be composed of deciduous vines and trees so that the sun will not be cut off from the patio and the house windows in the winter when its warmth will be welcome. Trees are an especially effective sun control device, since they shade the patio and protect the interior of the house from the sun's heat and may also shade the roof of the house and provide still another cooling effect. If the tree is to be located within the patio, please remember that paving can keep both air and water from reaching the roots. Use a porous paving such as brick in sand and do not pave the area close to the tree.

If there are existing trees, design the garden to utilize them to the fullest extent. Trees are so valuable a landscaping device that a large healthy tree materially enhances the value of a lot. In California a large live oak tree is considered to add one thousand dollars to the value of a building site. In New Mexico a lovely old cottonwood might similarly be considered a pearl without price. Other native shrubs and plants could also be incorporated into your landscaping.

I know a charming garden containing a wild pear thicket which the owners were wise enough to retain. When they begin construction of their house, a space was cleared large enough to allow a bedroom wing to thrust out into it so that the windows open into a shady bower in the summer and have a view made interesting by the pattern of branches and trunks in the winter. When those pear trees burst into bloom in the spring, that garden must be little short of spectacular.

A mature tree can form the focal point for your landscaping and set the scale for the rest of the garden. An architectural garden design will have an advantage here. Walls and other features can be built to the proper scale and the design will look finished when first installed. There will be no waiting until the new planting grows to the required scale for the tree.

If your garden is small, plan the landscaping around your large tree as if it were the corner of a much larger garden and suggest further vistas around the bend. This is a trick used by many designers. If your house is also small, you could scale the rest of the design to that, and thus emphasize the size of the tree and the diminutive scale of the house. The important thing is to establish a firm relationship between the tree and the rest of the garden design.

If you must plant young trees, keep in mind how large they will become. The Morine locust, for example, will grow to be a very large tree. This locust is very desirable. It is thornless, relatively quick growing, and can tolerate Southwestern soils and growing conditions. It is deep rooted and casts a rather light shade, so it can be used with lawns and in plantings. The immature tree has an interesting branching pattern. The mature tree grows to a shape similar to that of the large eastern elm tree.

Other desirable trees to use are included with the list of plant materials at the end of this chapter.

If you need shade quickly and cannot afford to buy a large tree, plant a clump of three or four smaller trees with their roots entwined. They will soon form a sizeable pool of shade. Under usual conditions you will want to space trees with their size at maturity in mind. The inevitable exception is the Santa Fe garden in which trees have been planted close together to simulate a small grove.

Third, outdoor living areas should have privacy. Entertaining and relaxing should not be done under the neighbors' scrutiny. Privacy from the street and from nearby houses should be considered as you locate your patio. The garage or carport might help to shelter or screen it. Hedges or fences are the usual solution. Do not be deceived into thinking that a hedge will be cheaper than a fence. Hedges need maintenance, weeding, watering, and fertilizing. They must grow for several years before they are large enough to be effective. Occasionally they die back or are attacked by pests.

Sometimes a strategically placed tree or a tall screen may provide privacy as well as a fence can with less expense and more originality. If you like the effect of masses of shrubbery, why not combine a hedge with fencing? A curve of arborvitæ at the end of a tall fence makes it seem less forbidding.

Photinia makes a tall informal hedge which has pleasing bronze tones. It is such a handsome evergreen that it should be used more as a specimen plant in Southwestern landscaping.

Pyracantha is another useful evergreen. It has white flowers and attractive red or orange berries. It can be pruned severely, but grows freely to form a straggly though impenetrable hedge. Pyracantha winterkills occasionally, being vulnerable not only to low temperatures but also to the hot winter sun and drying winds which deplete its moisture at a time when it receives little watering. The red berry variety seems to be less hardy than the orange. Pyracantha might also be espaliered against a privacy screen. It grows exhuberantly to heights of fifteen feet and covers a wide area if unrestrained by pruning. Too often its mature size is not considered when it is used in foundation plantings. It deserves a more imaginative treatment than it generally receives.

Arizona cypress makes a thick screen and grows quickly. It requires room. California privet and euonymus japonicus are semievergreens which can be trimmed into a formal hedge. Euonymus japonicus grows into a large shrub if untrimmed. I have seen it trained into an attractive open-headed multi-trunked tree shape.

Tamarisk, which now grows wild all over the state, is alkali and drought resistant. Its feathery foliage and pink blooms are attractive with adobes. Plant it as a tall privacy hedge or train it as a patio tree. It is considered messy as it drops twigs constantly. Another small tree which makes an effective hedge is the Russian Olive. It may be grown as a shrub or a small tree. There are small fragrant yellow flowers in the spring and a small hard fruit attractive to birds in the fall. Russian Olive is deciduous, but its branching pattern and its dark colored bark make it attractive in winter. It grows quickly under a variety of conditions.

As you study how to make your outdoor living area private and sketch various ideas, other design elements will suggest themselves. You begin to visualize the area paved with brick or with concrete, or perhaps you cast about for another form of surfacing.

A number of materials can be used for this purpose. One of the cheapest and most readily available of them is gravel. It can be applied directly to the ground or placed over plastic sheeting or building paper which hampers the growth of weeds in it. Half-inch gravel is perhaps more pleasant to walk on than the larger sizes. It is easy to weed and to rake if it becomes covered with leaves in the fall. Level and tamp the area to be surfaced. Do not use a thick layer of gravel. Roll it if possible. It will require some weeding and raking, and it is used most successfully with some kind of border to keep it within bounds.

Concrete is perhaps the most commonly used paving material for patio surfaces. Large slabs are difficult for the amateur to construct. If you have the paving done for you, be sure that the ground upon which the slab is poured is thoroughly dampened, that the concrete is thoroughly tamped, and that expansion joint is used to help prevent cracking. Keep the slab dampened for several days as an aid to proper curing. Concrete should not be poured in freezing weather.

Since a smooth uncolored concrete slab near the house tends to reflect heat and glare into the house, it should be wise to explore other ways of using it as surfacing. It combines readily with other paving materials such as asphalt and brick. It can be scratched, colored, brushed, and decorated with pebbles to give it more interest and texture.

The amateur can handle the pouring of small squares with an oiled form which can be used over and over. Only a small batch of concrete need be mixed at one time and may be mixed in a wheelbarrow. Paving composed of these squares can be interrupted with planting pockets which will make the paved area seem larger. They can be edged with brick. Plain and colored squares can be alternated. For an interesting textured surface, pour the squares in forms which have been lined with crumpled newspaper. Make them at least four inches thick. You can pour them in place or move them into position later and set in sand. Ten pound concrete pavers cast in interlocking shapes are available commercially. They are laid in sand like other patio bricks and can withstand heavy traffic when used as driveway pavers.

Hot mix asphalt cannot be installed by the handyman, but it should be considered when large areas are to be paved. If dry cement is brushed over it when it is first laid, it has a soft light-colored surface that reflects heat and looks much like concrete paving. It was used satisfactorily in our garden, installed over a compacted dirt base, to pave a large patio and drive way. It has not become sticky nor unduly hot in warm weather. There is less glare from it than there would have been from concrete. It has been durable under daily use, and there has been no penetration of weeds.

Cold asphalt mix can be used by the handyman. A most interesting paving can be constructed by laying asphalt down in strips or squares between wide strips of concrete. Use a heavy roller to compact it. A strong pattern like this would be appropriate only for large areas of paving.

Brick is probably the most commonly used paving material for adobe homes. It weathers handsomely and does not reflect the heat and glare of the sun as concrete does. Common brick will disintegrate in patios, so use a special patio brick. Even local hard-fired brick is not completely satisfactory in this respect. If you live near a brick kiln, you might investigate the use of the clinker bricks. They are hard but misshapen and give a cobblestone effect.

Bricks may be laid in sand or on cement with mortar. The cost is liable to be prohibitive unless you are willing to do the work yourself. As a do-it-yourself project it is not unduly expensive.

The foundation for bricks laid in mortar should be three or four inches thick with a roughened surface. Before laying the bricks, spread this foundation with a mixture of two parts sand and one part cement and sprinkle it down lightly. Lay the bricks tightly and fill the cracks with the dry sand and cement mixture, sweeping it in with a push broom. Hose thoroughly.

To lay bricks in sand, spread the sand no less than one nor more than three inches thick over the area to be surfaced. Use a long 2 x 4 as a screed to be pulled along two parallel headers which are 2 x 4's set at the height you want the foundation to be. This will pull the excess toward you and leave a smooth and level foundation behind it. The bricks are then placed close together on the sand in staggered rows or in a herringbone or basket weave pattern. Start laying at a straight edge or along a chalk line. Tamp the bricks gently so they are firmly set and will not wobble. When the brick have all been laid, brush loose sand over them to fill all the cracks. Paving in sand should have a solid edging of concrete, wood, or bricks set in mortar to keep the bricks from shifting.

Stabilized adobe bricks have been used as paving in California. It might be interesting to explore the possibilities of the concrete building block shaped and colored to resemble adobe which is now available. Set in sand, it might make a handsome patio floor. Ajuga, creeping phlox, dwarf alyssum, or thyme might be planted between the cracks or in planting pockets to soften the look of the paving.

Wooden rounds are occasionally used and should prove quite satisfactory for many purposes if they are not used in areas where they would be damp most of the time. To keep them from shifting, place them within a border. Rounds used as stepping stones will remain in place if they are cut twelve inches high and sunk deeply into the ground so that they project only an inch or two. For durability, treat them with creosote or other fence post preservatives.

We are warned against the use of large areas of paving because of the heat they will reflect and radiate. Intelligent use of sun control devices will keep paved areas from becoming so warm, however, and a brief hosing in the afternoon will cool them by evaporation. Since our nights are generally cool, the heat held by the paving does not increase our discomfort as it might if night temperatures remained high. The large amount of paving in our own garden has not been impractical or uncomfortable.

As you plan where to place the outdoor living area you will also begin to visualize the walls and fences which might be needed to give privacy. They are almost indispensable in landscaping a small city lot. It is important to make them at least six feet high if you want real privacy. This height makes an effective background for plantings. Some city ordinances may prohibit a fence or wall over six feet high on a side yard boundary. Check local regulations concerning the height permitted before you plan your garden.

A cinder block wall that is little more than waist high surrounds many a city lot. These must be raised in some way for privacy. We added redwood basket weave to one such wall. In another garden we ignored the wall entirely and built an eight-foot redwood fence well within the lot line to avoid local restrictions. Honeysuckle on a chain link fence makes an evergreen privacy screen.

In country areas where privacy is no object, a low wall or fence may provide a visual separation from the surrounding countryside and provide a pleasant sense of enclosure without sacrificing a view. A low adobe wall, a corral type fence, or a low rock rubble wall would be all that is needed.

Since walls and fences are an important part of garden architecture, they must be carefully designed and planted so that they will be handsome as well as functional. Block walls are often painted or plastered. You might add a course of decorative blocks or a brick coping at the top. They could be decorated with a cement sand casting or a panel of Mexican tile. Plant out parts of them so that they appear less forbidding. Try bush roses like Austrian Copper, espeliered pyracantha, or a handsome climbing rose. English ivy will eventually cover a wall with a northern exposure. Boston ivy is deciduous but has an interesting pattern of stems in winter. Try massing shrubbery in a corner and feature a small flowering tree or shrub, standing by itself, further along the wall where it can cast interesting shadows summer and winter.

Of course adobe walls enhance adobe houses as do rock rubble walls and *latia* fences of thin saplings bound together with wire. All look well with informal gardens. All will be relatively inexpensive if installed as a do-it-yourself project. A high adobe wall pierced with an opening covered by a wooden grill suggests seclusion yet allows a view of the world beyond the patio.

Walls not only insure privacy, but they also deflect the wind. They also deflect cooling breezes. A fence that is raised about twelve inches in posts or a slat fence may be better in some cases than a solid wall. This would be especially true if you are enclosing a small space. Studies made by the staff of *Sunset Magazine* seem to indicate that a slat fence gives better wind protection than a solid wall. It breaks the force of the wind without creating wind turbulence. The wind washes over a solid fence much as a wave breaks over a jetty. A forty-five degree baffle can be constructed on the wall to lift the wind in a gentle arc.

You often see low picket fences surrounding dooryard gardens in small mountain communities in New Mexico. The modern trend toward wooden fencing, however, is to build high, eye-stopping structures. Painted fences require constant maintenance in this climate, but stained wooden fences blend harmoniously with adobe exteriors. A fence of rough-sawed lumber, antiqued with a stain followed by a lightly sprayed coat of gray glaze (thinned oil paint) will look as if it had grown from a rustic site.

It is best to avoid busy or intricate designs for large areas of fencing. Building an attractive fence is well within the skill of the average handyman. Fence materials and fence sections can even be ordered by mail. Set fence posts in concrete and treat them with a preservative before they are installed. Adobe, rock, and block walls should be built on concrete foundations.

While you may have several choices in locating the outdoor living areas, the placement of the driveway will be more or less determined by the location of the garage or carport. In this day of two and often three-car families, some provision should also be made for off-the-street parking and, if possible, a place to turn around so that it is not necessary to back automobiles into the street. This is important if your have a hillside site. It takes room, for automobiles require space in which to maneuver. In the country your problem will be mainly one of design. In the city it will take careful planning to utilize the available space fully. Check city restrictions before you plan a street-side parking bay or loop driveway.

The turn-around loop is one device frequently used to provide off-the-street parking and drive-out ease. It can have a diameter of twenty-four feet, but if you want to have passing room beside parked cars, it should be sixteen feet wide and have a thirty-foot radius. Obviously, the loop is not practical on a narrow lot since it requires about seventy feet of frontage. Perhaps a neighbor would pave a section of his garden adjacent to yours to provide a combined turning space of workable size.

If you have a narrow lot and the set back is deep, it may be possible to make the front garden an entrance court, surfaced with paving or gravel, in which cars can be parked off the street. Parking space for each car should be ten feet wide. There must be approximately four feet between parked automobiles to permit passengers to get into and out of them comfortably. Diagonal parking bays use space thriftily. Parking space could be provided in back of the house. This makes a place where automobiles may be worked on out of sight of the street. It also tends to channel traffic through the back entry of the house.

Driveways and parking strips often pose special problems in planting. Plantings should be low to allow ease in opening automobile doors and an unrestricted view for the driver pulling into the street. One common problem spot is a narrow strip of land between the driveway and the lot line. It is frequently too hot and dry to grow much, takes abuse from traffic, and catches papers and leaves. Paving the driveway clear to the lot line removes the problem. Honeysuckle, vinca major or minor, or creeping rosemary can stand the abuse in such a spot.

Another problem is created by running the front walk to the house parallel with the driveway so that a narrow strip of ground is left between the two. Often the walk and drive could be combined in a design leading the eye toward the entrance and providing a paved entry area. To avoid a parking lot look, you might plan to use textured paving or introduce planting pockets.

Your main object in designing driveways and parking courts should be the convenience, comfort, and safety of your family and guests, If driveways do not function well, there is little point to having them at all. Lay them out with stakes and string to be sure the turning radius is adequate and that there is enough space to maneuver in comfortably. Make provisions for good night lighting. If space and the budget permit, you might plan for shelter from the weather for those entering or leaving automobiles at the main entrance.

Driveways and motor courts may make a fine place for roller skating and bike riding for the small fry, but if possible play areas for children should be separated from them. It is not necessary to leave a screened-off no man's land for the children's garden. They appreciate garden beauty as much as adults, and children and flowers can grow happily in the same garden with a little advance planning for the protection of both.

Flowers could be placed in raised beds where they will be seen and enjoyed (and easily weeded) but will still be protected from tricycle wheels. Grass will not take the abuse it would receive under swing sets and jungle gyms. Plan to have some surfaced area for playground equipment. Even a small square of paving provides a place for tetherball, hopscotch, jacks, marbles, trucks, and dolls. Sand boxes may become flower boxes when the children outgrow them. A wide ledge serves to confine the sand to the box . . . more or less. Play areas for small children should be fenced for safety, shaded for comfort, and easily supervised from the house.

It is not wise to combine the play area with a service area where clotheslines, garbage cans, garden work centers, and tool storage are located.

Plan as carefully for the service area as for other sections of the garden. It can be convenient and attractive. Provide for the safe storage of poison sprays and sharp tools out of children's reach.

Clotheslines should be convenient to the laundry. In small gardens they might be retractable or the umbrella type which come equipped with a canvas cover and double as a garden umbrella.

Construct compost bins so that compost can be easily worked every few days. Raw compost should be at a five-foot level which will allow optimum heat to build up and yet permit the proper distribution of air and water to insure quick composting without odor or flies. Cold frames should be located to take advantage of the early spring sun. Elaborate service areas may have a lath house or a small greenhouse. On the other hand, some families will merely need room for a garbage can and a corner in the garage for the lawn mower.

Make the service area readily accessible from other parts of the garden. You should be able to move freely from any part of the garden

Simple gate in a mud plaster wall. Gale garden.

Handsome gate stands slightly ajar to welcome the visitor into a small entrance court. Well designed planter featuring a single small juniper is the only embellishment this entrance needs. Mud plaster, two types of paving, and the texture of the gate are used to add interest. Nat Kaplan, designer.

Good garden architecture: brick paving, interesting doorway. Hopkins garden.

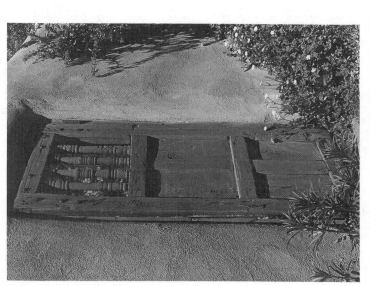

Handsome doorway enhances the lovely Edwards garden, Santa Fe.

The owner carved these inviting gates. Kimmons garden.

High adobe wall and deeply shadowed archway are in a scale compatible with a large home.

Morgan, Ludlow garden, Santa Fe.

Brick paving laid in sand forms a driveway. Here bricks are being laid on edge for greater durability. Pattern is alternated for more interest.

Change in levels adds interest to large expanse of patio paving in the Hopkins garden. Note that the plantings are placed away from the vulnerable adobe walls.

Garden ornaments do not need to be man made. Here a planting of cactus in a weathered log is used with great effect. Shreve garden.

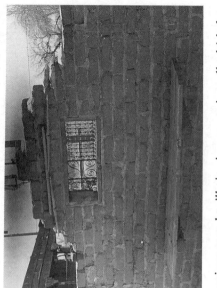

Antique metal grille is nice accent in wall which features bench on either side bolted to supports running through the wall.

Ornament on the garden wall of the Urton home Sandoval.

Pottery in an effective setting.

Pottery crafted by the owner is a handsome garden accessory. Casteel garden.

Plants in this courtyard garden can be enjoyed from almost every room in the house. McKee home, Sandoval.

Handcrafted pottery again as effective accessory.

Old grinding stone is used to ornament the Edwards garden.

Poles with the bark left on form a "shade" over a semicircle paved with sections of railroad ties grouted with cement. Color, texture, pattern of light and shadows are very pleasing. DeWerd garden, Corrales.

to another. Traffic can be channeled by the way in which walks and pathways are laid out.

Stepping stones, concrete circles of various sizes, wood rounds, and an infinite variety of forms and surfacing materials can be used which will be in keeping with the design of the garden. Make walks simple and straightforward. Their function is to get you from here to there. They should be attractive but not distracting. Plan them as an integral part of your garden design.

It is not cheap to build this kind of garden. Paving, walks, walls, and fences represent a big investment in materials and labor. At first glance it may seem almost prohibitive. Keep in mind that it is an investment, enhancing not only your enjoyment of your property but also its market value. For this reason banks and other lending agencies are willing to make loans for landscaping. They will want a plan, drawn to scale, showing what improvements you plan to make. A nurseryman or landscaping contractor can assist you in making out your application.

This emphasis on garden structure does not mean that the selection of plant material can be a secondary consideration. Each plant is selected for its contribution to the total design.

Do not be alarmed if this seems to call for more knowledge of plants than you feel you possess. Although a bewildering variety of shrubs, trees, vines, bulbs, and flowers are available at the nurseries, your own garden can contain only a relatively small number of them. If you learn all you can about those which you decide to plant, what sun, soil, and water they require, what their mature size will be, and what sort of root structure they have, you can design and maintain plantings as handsome as those of the professional gardener or landscaper.

To help the novice or the newcomer to the state select plants for each spot in his garden, a list of plants which grow well in New Mexico is included at the end of this chapter. Special attention has been given to natives. While some have difficulty in irrigated gardens, many others will thrive under irrigation. Native plants make handsome low maintenance gardens especially suitable for adobe homes.

Unfortunately there are few public gardens in the state where you can study plants and learn their growth habits and their ultimate size and shape. What a surprise it is when the tiny evergreen brought in from the foothills develops into a monster which cracks the foundation and overpowers the house. I recently saw a juniper which had grown so large that its owner had cut an arched passageway through it to reach his front door.

How are we to learn? One way is to take a drive in older neighborhoods where the gardens are mature. You will see that the little sprig of pyracantha you saw in a gallon can at the nursery will grow in a surprisingly short time into a thorny giant higher than a house. Pfitzer junipers reach spreads of over six feet in a few years. Notice how tall an untrimmed euonymus japonicus will grow. These are three shrubs commonly found in New Mexico gardens, often planted with little thought to their size at maturity.

Talk to your gardening friends. Ask the names of plants which you like. Question the nursery salesperson. Consult your county extension agent. You can join a garden club or take a short course in landscaping. In 1964 a short course in landscaping and plant ecology was offered at New Mexico State University under the sponsorship of the garden clubs of the state.

You will find that you learn a lot about Southwestern gardening just by keeping your eyes open as you drive about. You will notice that English Ivy thrives in a northern exposure. Santolina will grow in a hot, dry location which would discourage many plants. You may be surprised to see an exotic magnolia in an Albuquerque garden, and you will be heartened to see the old favorites from "back home" like lilacs, roses, iris, and bridal wreath growing happily. You'll look in vain for acid loving azalea or rhododendron. You will see how much we must water our gardens. Above all, I hope that you will see enough good gardens to encourage you to proceed with plans for your own with great interest and enthusiasm.

A major fault of much amateur landscaping is combining too many kinds of plants. Natural settings do not contain one each of a variety of plants. A few plants with similar requirements occur over and over. Yet natural landscapes are not monotonous or uninteresting, though a restful unity pervades them.

It is also a common fault to plant too much and too close together. Landscaping which is done with no thought of the ultimate size and shape of quick growing plants in it will soon be disappointing. It is better to space trees and shrubs correctly and fill in with annuals and perennials until the planting matures.

I do not mean to imply that some alteration of the garden planting will not become necessary. Shrubs will get leggy and need replacing. As trees grow and cast more shade, some reworking of the beds will be inevitable. However, a good garden has a long range plan which takes into consideration the growth patterns of the plants selected for it.

Another thing often overlooked in amateur gardens is the interplay of color and texture. Green leaves are not just green but yellow green or greyed green or bronze green. Not all greens look pleasing together. Plants which like hot, dry locations are often grey green in color: chamisa, santolina, cotoneaster. Plants which like wet or shady spots are often yellow green. In many instances plants not only do not look pleasing together, but they do not do well under the same growing conditions.

You can use the reddish foliage of the purple plum (Cistena or Hansen) the red leaf crab, the andorra juniper, and nandina for interest and variation in the garden color scheme. The bronze color of the new growth on Photinia is lovely.

Shiny leaves reflect light. Dull leaves absorb it. Some leaves are opaque and some are translucent.

Variety in leaf textures also adds interest. Textures range from the fineness of lawn to the coarseness of catalpa leaves. In massed plantings, fine textures should predominate, while coarse leaves add contrast and points of interest. Bamboo, nandina, cutleaf maple, Persian lilac, cotoneaster, and bridal wreath have fine-textured foliage. Mahonia, photinia, castor bean have large leaves.

The shape, branching pattern, and color of bark of the deciduous trees and shrubs will be an important design element in winter. Evergreens give year round color. A preponderance of coniferous evergreens may look a bit somber. We are very fortunate that our climate, except in mountain areas, permits us to use broadleaf evergreens. Be careful not to use too many conifers with a pointed or conical shape. The dark tone of the foliage and the strong vertical line distract the eye like exclamation marks on a printed page. For a natural effect try massing broadleaf evergreens and then underplant, placing low growing plants at the base of the taller ones. Once it is established, a mass planting will require little care.

Use flowers for color accents in permanent plantings rather than planting them in beds unless you are a dedicated gardener and enjoy the work and planning involved in keeping a bed pretty and colorful all season. Flowering trees and shrubs can be used for color as well as bedding plants. Use quince, forsythia, redbud, crab, roses, rose acacia, Spanish broom, and crepe myrtle, to name a few. Surprising as it may seem, not all flower colors go well together. You can select a color scheme for your garden just as you select a color scheme for your living room.

I hope that I have convinced you that there is more to selecting plants for your garden than a Saturday afternoon trip to the nursery for a few shrubs. Not only is it important to select the type of plant with the right requirements for soil, water, and sunlight and the right ultimate size and shape, a compatible color and the proper leaf texture for a given spot, but you must select the right individual plant.

Not any redbud will do for that spot by the front door. It may call for a multi-trunked tree. If the branches arch, they should arch toward rather than away from the doorway. In another spot, a little round headed tree may be better. Suppose a tree has a low branch, and that cutting it off would spoil the tree's shape. Don't hope that as the tree grows this branch will grow higher. If it is too low now, it will always be too low.

Do not select an upright, leggy shrub for underplanting but look for one which already has a layered look. If you want to train a pyracantha against a wall, look for a plant with only a few main stems and an interesting branching pattern. Perfectly symmetrical plants are often not what you want; yet they are often more expensive at the nursery.

Most of the common annuals and perennials will do well here. Aster, gaillardia, columbine (in shade), day lily, pink, flax, hollyhock, oriental poppy, phlox, creeping phlox, shasta daisy, red hot poker, violet, and wallflower are easily grown perennials. Cosmos, four-o-clock, balsam, larkspur, morning-glory, marguerite, petunia, and zinnia are annuals which are commonly seen. As I write this list I think of the colorful dooryard gardens, a jumble of many of these old favorites, behind a low fence adding a splash of color to the dooryards of the little adobes along country roads.

The list at the end of this chapter includes ground covers. In difficult areas they are very useful. By far the most popular ground cover, however, is grass. The most handsome lawns are perhaps those of

Merion or Kentucky Blue. Some gardeners prefer a mixture of grasses and clover, feeling that a mixture means less chance for a completely denuded lawn when disease or drought strike. Rye can make an attractive lawn. It is sometimes used for a temporary lawn and plowed under when a permanent lawn is seeded. If you are considering planting Bermuda, my advice would be "don't." Once planted, it is impossible to eradicate completely. It is slow to green up in the spring and quick to turn brown in the fall. Contrary to popular notion, it requires periodic feeding and mowing. Any lawn is going to require some work and attention. With a little more effort you can maintain a lawn of Merion or Kentucky Blue.

Many lawn problems seem to stem from a heavy clay soil which is easily compacted and has a slow water absorption rate. Deep and thorough watering, rather than frequent sprinklings, and periodic feedings will keep grass healthy and pest and disease resistant. Do not mow blue grass short, but leave stems about two inches long. Catch the clippings but DON'T put them in the garbage can. If you are a Saturday afternoon gardener with no interest in a compost bin, use the clippings as a mulch around trees, shrubs, and flowers. This keeps down weeds, conserves moisture, and keeps a hard crust from forming which will keep necessary air from the plant roots. Grass clippings contain nitrogen and may add a little badly needed humus to the soil.

Humus improves both clay and sandy soils and tends to combat alkalinity. Like most soils in areas of scanty rainfall, Southwestern soils are generally alkaline. You will not need to add lime to such soils. When there is an excess of lime, plants may suffer from a form of chlorosis. Leaves turn yellow, while the veins remain green. If the condition is severe, the leaves develop brown edges and will eventually die. Peat moss is a valuable soil additive and tends to increase soil acidity.

Southwestern soil and climate pose special garden problems. Unless you love to garden, why fight it by trying to grow tender or acid-loving plants? Select from the number of handsome plant materials that tolerate alkaline conditions, low humidity, and drying winds. Handsome gardens will result if you learn a few tricks.

Learn to mulch heavily, to water deeply but not too frequently, to use a fertilizer manufactured to meet local soil conditions, to water during the winter, to pre-water and mix peat moss into deeply dug planting holes when transplanting. Plant spring-flowering bulbs almost twice as deep as in other areas and do not plant them where they get the south sun. Do not constantly stir up the soil. Instead of conserving moisture, this process actually speeds up the loss of moisture.

Easy does it. Hose plants with cold water early in the day to control aphids, spider mite, and mildew. Use a root feeder to water trees and shrubs. Carry pruning shears whenever you go into the garden. Clipping a twig here and there where it is needed will result in well-shaped plants without a drastic pruning session later. Plant bare root stock where possible to avoid introducing pests into your garden from the soil of canned stock. Pull weeds as they sprout, and no extensive weeding sessions will be necessary. Cutting off roses as they fade to the first five-leaf stem prunes the bush as well as removing the faded bloom. You can shape the bush at the same time. Cut above a five-leaf stem on the inside of the shoot if you wish upright shoots to grow to correct a too spreading shape. Avoid hedges which require trimming, small lawn areas which require hand clipping, herbaceous borders instead of permanent plantings. If you're the very relaxed type, you might even carry things to the extreme of planting plastic grass sold in rolls by Sears Roebuck. Or perhaps, like Mary Quite Contrary, you could grow a row of silver bells and cockleshells.

Indeed, like Mary's more and more Southwestern gardens feature some sort of garden ornament: an interesting rock, a weathered log, a piece of sculpture, a sand casting, wood carvings, a paneled or carved gate, a weathered bench in a sunny spot against an adobe wall.

If the landscape design is simple and structural, this garden ornament may be large and important and serve as a focal point for the whole garden. It might be an ornate fountain in a walled patio or a fresco on a protected wall. If native plantings carry the surrounding countryside right to the front door, something weathered and informal would be appropriate. Use an old grain chest on the *portál* or an old watering trough planted with succulents. Accessories will be successful only if they are compatible with the character of the garden. They can be dramatic or understated. Choose each piece because it is beautiful and appropriate. Avoid the coy, the cute, and the obvious. And remember you can have too much of even a good thing.

Garden furniture should be functional, well made, and simple in design. Expanded metal or redwood are more durable than canvas or plastic webbing, but the latter have the advantage of easy winter storage. Stack cushions, chair pillows, and pads for lounges may introduce a bright note of color. Above all, garden furniture must be comfortable, for today's garden is meant to be lived in. Have many, many happy hours in yours!

PLANT LIST

Note: Gardeners in northern New Mexico will find the plant list in Kelly's *Good Gardens in the Sunshine States* helpful. He lists materials suitable for Colorado gardens with growing conditions similar to those in northern New Mexico; similarly, growing conditions of like kind in other states are suitable for this list.

TREES

**Suited to hot, dry locations.

Arizona Cypress (Cupressus Arizonica): Fast growing evergreen with shallow roots and spreading growth habit. Grey-green foliage. Can be grown in irrigated areas. Will not tolerate prolonged low temperatures. Grows to about thirty feet.**

Green ash (Fraxinus pennsylvania lanceolata): Grows slowly and casts dense shade. Hardy and drought resistant.**

Hackberry (Celtis occidentalis): Leaf similar to elm leaf. Grows quickly. Subject to gall. Tolerates alkaline soil. Drought resistant. Dark red "berries."

Moraine locust (Gleditsia triacanthos inermis moraine): Fine leaves and light shade. Thornless, seedless, deep rooted. Grows quite rapidly to large size. Long-lived and drought resistant.

Mulberry (Morus alba): Fruitless variety is fast growing and well adapted to alkaline soil, heat, and drought. Large leaves and dense shade. Branches brittle in high winds.**

Pinon pine (Pinus edulis): Slow growing, irregularly shaped native which can be trained to stay small indefinitely. Sold balled and burlapped.**

Ponderosa pine (Pinus ponderosa): Native which will tolerate drought. Requires room. Somewhat difficult to transplant.

Russian olive (Eleagnus augustifolia): Small to medium size with informal shape and narrow silvery leaves. Casts light shade and is deep rooted. Salt tolerant and alkali resistant but does not thrive in acid soils. Small flowers in May followed by small hard fruits relished by birds. Excellent honey source. Hardy and pest free. Withstands temperature from 50 degrees below zero to 115 degrees above.**

Siberian elm (Ulmus pumila): Large tree. Vase shape. Hardy and quick growing. Easy to transplant. Its shallow root system and countless seeds make it objectionable in small gardens.**

Silk tree (Albizzia julibrissin): Sometimes called mimosa in error. Tropical appearance. Low branching habit and spreading head. Pink blossoms in June, July, and August. Hardy, fast growing. Will stand alkaline soil. Not for most northern gardens.

Tree of Heaven ailanthus (Ailanthus altissima): Tree growing freely in New Mexico. Considered weedy. Suckers from roots. Extremely hardy. Tolerates poor soil and growing conditions. Attractive foliage. Male tree has bad odor.**

Western broadleaf Cottonwood (Populus Sargenti): The big cottonwood on the stream banks. Females produce cotton. Hardy and pest free and grows under difficult conditions if it gets plenty of water.

Western catalpa (Catalpa speciosa): Beautiful large tree with big leaves, handsome flowers, and seed pods. No serious pests.

Western Red Cedar (Juniperus scapulorum): Native to state and good in all areas. Small blue berries. Grows to about forty feet.**

Willows (Salix): Undesirable as garden trees. Brittle, short lived, and greedy feeders who rob other plants. Roots clog sewers.

SMALL TREES

Arborvitae (Thuja) Compact and slow growing. Dwarf forms reach three to four feet (Bonita and Berkmans Golden) while others grow to thirty feet. Some varieties turn brown or yellow in winter. Can be trimmed and shaped.

Crepe myrtle (Lagerstroemia indica): Tall shrub which can be trained into small multi-trunked tree. Dark green, glossy leaves and long lasting pink, red, rose, or lavender flowers. Slow growing. Likes sun. May winterkill at lower temperatures unless in protected spot. Not for northern New Mexico.

Flowering crabapple (Malus): Bechtel, Eley, Red Silver, and Hopa are best known varieties. Eley is spreading. Hopa is slender. Some subject to blight. Showy pink blossoms in spring. Roots do not rob other plantings. Bechtel has no fruit.

Flowering plum (Prunus cerasifera pissardi): Reddish foliage and pink blossoms in spring. Upright shape.

Goldenrain tree (Koelreuteria paniculata): Handsome small tree with fine leaves. Mature tree has high arching head. Yellow flowers in June and July followed by interesting fruits. Slow growing and will kill back in the northern half of the state. Tolerates drought and alkaline soil.**

Japanese tree lilac (Syringa japonica): Small tree or tall shrub with white flowers in June. Slow growing and hardy.

Redbud (Cercis canadensia): Dark bark and branching pattern attractive in winter. Purple-pink flowers early in spring. Leaves subject to wind damage. Rather hard to transplant.

Staghorn sumac (Rhus typhina): Small tree or tall shrub with interesting open shape. Short lived and shallow rooted but valuable for its interesting appearance.**

Tamarisk (Tamarix pentandra): Grows as shrub or can be trained as informal small tree. Widespread throughout New Mexico since introduction at turn of century by Department of Agriculture. Easy to propagate and very hardy. Thrives in heat, low humidity, and alkaline soil. Will grow in irrigated gardens. Foliage grey where it gets little water, bright green elsewhere. Trunk is shaggy. Foliage fine and featherly like juniper. Long sprays of pink flowers in early summer. Somewhat messy.**

TALL SHRUBS

Algerita (Berberis haematocarpa): Large evergreen grows in southern part of state. Leaves are compound and leaflets look like holly leaves. Fragrant small yellow flowers in May and June followed by red berries good for jelly. Secondary host for black stem rust of cereals.**

Apache plume (Fallugia Paradoza): Found at elevations up to 7,000 feet. Drought resistant native which will grow in irrigated gardens. Fuzzy, twisted seed heads follow white rose-like flowers about the size of apple blossoms.

Bamboo: Hardiness varies with species. Chinese Goddess grows to six feet. Hardy to 20 degrees. Airy look and fine leaf. Tall hedge bamboo hardy to about 16 degrees.

Chamisa (Atriplex canescens): Tall grey native shrub found all over the state. Often erroneously called sage. Small blooms in clusters in middle of summer followed by small fruit which remain on plant well into winter. Hardy, drought resistant. Tolerates cold. Can be transplanted when small or grown from seed. Little care needed when established.**

Creosote bush (Larrea divaricata): Evergreen native with dark green leaves which give off an odor like creosote when wet. Yellow blossoms in early spring followed by fuzzy seed balls. Grows rapidly in irrigated gardens. Hard to transplant. Called Little Stinker (*bediondilaa*) by the Mexicans. Leaves are covered with a "varnish" which conserves moisture.**

Desert willow (Chilopsis linearis): Not a true willow but has leaves resembling willow leaves. Large purplish or white flowers mottled with dots and splashes of brown. Blooms profusely. Can be trained as a small informal tree where it gets water in an irrigated garden. Easily transplanted. Available in some nurseries and as a native shrub. Grows in the arroyas and foothills of the mountains at lower elevations, and is found usually below 4,000 feet from West Texas to California. Some handsome specimens can be seen thriving in Albuquerque gardens. A very handsome and valuable shrub.**

Euonymus japonicus: Grows at moderate rate to heights of fifteen feet but can be severely pruned and trimmed. Is semi-evergreen. Has glossy green foliage. Subject to hard-to-control scale. Can tolerate a dry, sunny location. Winterkills in Santa Fe.

Forsythia (Forsythia intermedia spectabilis): Quick growing upright shrub, rather uninteresting except in early spring when it is covered with yellow blooms. Forsythia suspensa has a drooping growth habit.

Fountain butterfly bush (Buddleia alternifolia): Tall shrub with loose growth habit and long spikey lavender flower stems in summer. Easy to grow. Not hardy but will send up new shoots which will bloom in summer even if it winterkills.

Hansens purple plum (Prunus cistena): Handsome red foliage and small white flowers in the spring. Grows slowly to about ten feet. Has spreading open head.

Lilac (Syringa vulgaris): This old favorite seems to grow everywhere. Do not over-fertilize. Hardy and blooms profusely in early spring.

Ocotillo (Fouquierie splendens): Long spines grow from several tall stems. Brilliant scarlet flowers in spring. Fine specimen for cactus garden.**

Oregon grape (Mahonia aquifolium): Useful broadleaf evergreen seems to thrive in any exposure. Foliage is glossy and a dark green and new growth is bonzy. Some red leaves appear in winter. Leaves look like holly leaves. The bloom is yellow followed by small dark blue fruit. Grows in tall informal shape. A form said to stay within three to six feet is now available. Moderate to rapid growth.

Pampas grass (Cortaderia argintea): Grows in large clump and produces tall showy plumes in fall. Drought resistant. Not hardy without protection in cold climate.

Photinia: Broadleaf evergreen with large shiny leaves. New foliage is bronze color. Moderate rate of growth to fifteen feet. Spreading growth habit. Will suffer from hot winter sun unless it receives some winter watering. Not for Santa Fe but grows well in Albuquerque.

Poinciana (Caesalpinia gillessi): Large showy flowers with yellow petals and red stamens followed by large seed pods. Fine foliage on green sparingly branched stems. Hardy and drought resistant. Can be grown as far north as Albuquerque.**

Pyracantha: Tall thorny shrub also known as firethorn. Small white flowers in clusters followed by bright red or orange berries. Glossy evergreen leaves. Quick growing. Can be sheared or trained as an espelier. Occasionally seen trimmed in pom pom shapes at the end of a few heavy branches. Untrimmed it makes a large thick straggly shrub which grows to heights of fifteen feet.

Roseacaia (Robinia hispida): Locust with informal shape and beautiful pink pea-like flowers in clusters. Suckers freely. Can be grafted to make a small tree with a straight trunk and a spreading bushy head.

Rose of Sharon (Hibicscus syriacus): Sometimes called shrub althea. Grows to height of ten feet. Attractive flowers in late summer.

Spanish broom (Genista hispanica): Finely branched and almost devoid of leaves. Very fragrant yellow pea-like flowers in summer. Grows thick and bushy to about eight feet. Drought resistant and hardy to about 10 degrees.**

Yellow elder (Tecoma stans): Native found in southern New Mexico. Easily propagated. Showy yellow flowers. Fast growing.

Yucca Elata: New Mexico state flower. Has beautiful creamy white flowers on tall stalks followed by interesting seed pods. Requires sandy, gravely soil.

SHRUBS TO SIX FEET

Cliffrose (Cowania mexicana): Native with interesting gnarled and twisted shape and white flowers which look like wild roses and smell like orange blossoms. May grow to ten feet.**

Cotoneaster: Ornamental shrubs useful in massed plantings. Parnay is evergreen with red berries. Good for southern gardens. Divaricata is tall and spreading with large red berries. Necklace is low and spreading with evergreen leaves. Freeze back in northern New Mexico.

Fendler bush (Fendlera rupicola): Attractive native which resembles the mockorange. Showy and fragrant white flowers.

Nandina (Nandina domestica): Not a bamboo but often called Sacred Bamboo. Has a similar light, airy appearance. Grows slowly to about six feet. Foliage turns red in winter. Clusters of red berries. Likes a warm spot but will tolerate some shade. Not for northern gardens but does well in Albuquerque.

New Mexico buckeye (Ungnadia speciosa): Easily transplanted native. Reddish stems and compound leaves. Clusters of pink flowers in early spring. Seed pod resembles buckeye. New Mexico State horticulturists recommend shade if it is planted in southern New Mexico. Transplants quite well. Found in the foothills of the drier mountains.

Pfitzer juniper (Juniperus chinensis pfitzeriana): Spreading evergreen which grows rapidly to spreads of fifteen feet. Grows well in sun or shade. Can be sheared or pruned, but do not try to keep under six feet in width. Virtually pest free.

Quince (Chaenomeles japonica): Slow growing deciduous shrub with bright orange-red flowers in early spring on leafless branches. Subject to chlorosis. Selected specimens can be trained flat against a wall in an informal shape.

Redleaf Japanese barberry (Berberis thunbergi atropurpurea): An upright stiff shrub with thorny branches. Foliage stays red all summer. Grows slowly to medium height. Stands shearing and can be used in a clipped hedge.

Roses: All types grow well in New Mexico. Require deep watering about once a week. Humus should be worked into soil when roses are planted and an organic mulch used around them. Fertilize after each blooming. Floribundas give good massed effects.

Shrub roses (Rosa foetida): Large drooping shrubs that bloom only once. Very hardy. Austrian Copper and Harison Yellow are good varieties.**

Sergeant's barberry (Berberis sargenti): Slow growing barberry with glossy yellow green foliage on stiff thorny branches. There are yellow flowers in early spring, but they are inconspicuous. Good in massed planting.

Spirea or bridal wreath (Spirea prunifolia): Large deciduous shrub with arching spreading branches loaded with white blooms in May. Prune by cutting out old stems to the ground. Do not shear off top as is often done.

Squawbush (Rhus trilobata): Member of the sumac family which grows as far north as Canada. This native is valuable for fall color. Sticky orange-red berries are edible. Wide irregular branching habit.

GROUND COVERS

English ivy (Eldera helix): Large leaf. Evergreen vine which can be used as ground cover in shaded areas. Likes northern exposure.

Halls Japanese honeysuckle (Lonicera heckrotti): High mounding ground cover or vine, holds its leaves through the winter. White flowers in late spring. Will climb into shrubs. Grows exhuberantly. Can tolerate a hot, sunny location.**

Junipers: Several low junipers make good ground covers. Bar Harbor, Andorra, Waukegan, and Tamarix are some examples. All grow well in ordinary soil with little care. Space at least three feet apart.**

Mahonia repens: A prostrate form of oregon grape which will require some shade. This native grows very low. Foliage, fruit, and flowers like those of Mahonia aquifolium.

Prostrate rosemary (Rosemarianus officinalis protratus): An evergreen shrub with narrow aromatic leaves and tiny blue flowers in late fall. Can be used in a hot, dry location in poor or average soil. Winters as far north as Albuquerque in sheltered location.

Santolina (Santolina chamaecyparissus): Aromatic shrub with greyish foliage and small round yellow flowers. Grows well in hot dry location. Occasionally winterkills. Must be replaced about every four years. Easily sheared as a small formal hedge around flower beds. Loose open growth if not sheared. Useful plant.**

Vinca minor: Sometimes called periwinkle. Evergreen ground cover. Spreads rapidly in a dense mat. Small blue flowers in spring. Vinca Major has a larger leaf and flower. Both grow very exhuberantly. Vinca Major will grow into shrubs, is sometimes difficult to control in beds with other plantings.

Wintercreeper (Euonymus fortunei radicans): Evergreen vine which also runs along the ground in a thick mat. Will grow in sun or shade. A hardy and desirable plant. Will grow up on walls and fences without support.

APPENDIX

Forms for adobe bricks. Note hand holds at sides. Mold may be lined with sheet metal to keep mud from clinging to it as it is lifted off of the bricks. Form at the top is for half and quarter size bricks. The size of adobes is not standard. The Albuquerque Building Code requires a minimum size of 4x10x14 inches. Bricks this size weigh close to 35 pounds, and it will take roughly 1 cubic yard of dirt for each 100 adobes. Making your own is not for the faint-hearted. 11,000 adobes will be needed for a 2,000 square foot house with 14 inch walls.

If a mechanical mixer is used, it should be a plaster mixer with paddles which scrape the sides rather than a cement mixer. Bricks should not be made during freezing or rainy weather. They will disintegrate if they freeze or are soaked before curing. They must cure before being laid up in a wall. The Albuquerque Code requires at least three weeks of curing. A thoroughly dry adobe will be a uniform color all the way through.

Block presses such as the Cinva Ram are available which mold a strong and uniform brick, but production is slower than casting the mud in forms by hand.

Sketch of footing and foundation showing minimum requirements for normal soils. If fill has been used on the site, footings must be placed on undisturbed soil. It is wise to check local conditions with someone who has built in the area. If soil is of low load bearing capacity wider footings will be needed.

Footings can be poured in a trench dug into firm earth with a straight sided shovel. Dampen the trench before pouring. Foundation forms should be firmly nailed and braced to withstand the weight of wet concrete. If hollow concrete bricks are used to build the foundation fill the top course with concrete. Use 2000-pound concrete if you use transit mix. Do-it-yourself concrete should be 1 part cement, 3 parts sharp (not water worn) sand, and 4 parts 1½" aggregate. Do not use more than six gallons of water per sack of cement.

Concrete poured in the winter must not be allowed to freeze. Do not place concrete on a frozen base. Heat the materials. The concrete should be between 50 and 70 degrees F when poured. Protect the concrete with an inch thick layer of straw or with canvas to keep temperatures from dropping below 70 degrees for three days or 50 degrees for five days. Temperatures 40 degrees and below will slow the rate at which concrete sets.

Chemical additives to prevent freezing affect the strength and other properties of concrete adversely. Use accelerators cautiously. Calcium chloride, one of the most common, should be added in solution to the water used in mixing. If it comes in contact with the cement a flash may occur. Use no more than two pounds of calcium chloride per bag of cement. Using high-early-strength Portland cement increases the setting rate and strength development, reducing the time that protection must be supplied. Too rapid drying in hot weather also lowers the strength of concrete. Keep it moist at least 5 days after pouring.

CONCRETE FOR FOOTINGS

Height	Width	Cubic yards concrete per foot of length
8"	12"	.0247
10	10	.0255
10	12	.0308
12	12	.0370
12	14	.0432
12	16	.0492
12	18	.0555
12	20	.0618
12	22	.0677
12	24	.0740

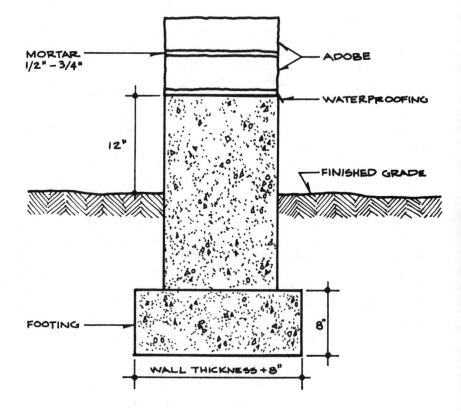

MORTAR
1/2" – 3/4"

ADOBE

WATERPROOFING

12"

FINISHED GRADE

FOOTING

8"

WALL THICKNESS + 8"

Stabilized adobes which have been in place in an outside wall for nine years. The soil was not screened. Check with local building supervisors before making your own stabilized adobes as some codes require prior approval for the use of hardeners or stabilizers. An acceptable brick can be made with as little as 2% by weight asphalt emulsion or high asphalt content crude oil. The latter is inferior to the emulsion but is much cheaper. On cold days warm the emulsifier before using.

The most important step in the making of stabilized adobes is the mixing of raw materials. Mix asphalt and water and add the soil gradually until the proper consistency is reached. If straw is added to help the brick shrink and dry as one unit use short 2 to 6 inch lengths and add at the end of mixing. Pigment powders for cement can be added to stabilized bricks.

Asphalt stabilized adobes can be laid up with a mortar of mud the same composition as the bricks, cement mortar, or a mixture of one part Portland cement, 1 part lime, and no more than 6 volumes of sand.

Plumbing is roughed in before the walls go up. Water and drainage pipes should not be enclosed in adobe walls unless the bricks are stabilized. Utility pipes or conduit up to an inch in diameter can be set into grooves cut into adobe walls. Walls can be thickened to install larger pipes. Steel pipe should not be laid underground or buried under concrete floors. Roughing in includes the installation and test of the pipes for the water supply and drainage system. Installation must conform to applicable state, county, and city plumbing codes. Unless the system is properly designed there could be cross connections between the water supply system and other piping, back siphonage from a fixture into the water supply system, or leaks in the drainage system through which sewage or gases could escape.

Every fixture must be trapped and vented. Traps prevent dangerous sewer gases from backing up through open drain fixtures. A soil pipe into which the water closet drains is connected with the main building drain and is vented up through the roof to the outside air. You can plan the location of other fixtures so that all or most can be vented through stack. The waste disposal system is generally a gravity system, so the size and the slope of the drain pipe must be adequate to get a good flow.

An adobe addition going up. Mortar is shoveled onto the wall ahead of the brick layer and the adobes are set into place. Note that the windows are being set as the walls go up. An optional method is to set the walls to rough bucks and place windows later as in plate #6. Cummings home, Albuquerque.

Detail of window installation. In the foreground a concrete window sill has been poured in forms on the wall.

Fireplace goes up as walls go up. Here fireplace is being constructed in the corner of double course walls. Adobes and stabilized adobe bricks should not be exposed directly to heat. Fireplace should be lined with fire brick.

Patio fireplace under construction at the Richard Sandoval home. The area of the fireplace opening is the same as the area of the firebox floor.

Detail showing lintel set in place over doorway in a double course wall. Lintels should extend at least twelve inches on either side of the opening. Concrete lintels may be poured in place on an adobe wall. Waterproof paper should be placed between the concrete and the bricks. For large spans the size of the lintel must be carefully determined for the load it will bear. It is necessary to leave clearance to allow for settling between the lintel and the head of the window or door frame. Three quarters of an inch is recommended. When there are several window openings and the distance between them is less than 24 inches, a lintel should carry the load across both the openings for the windows and the wall between them.

Fireplace completed and ready for plaster. Note concrete block footing visible at the left. Brick floors have been laid before plastering. A thick layer of fine sand will protect the surface while the walls are finished.

Electric wiring is placed in grooves in the adobe walls.

Roof vigas or rafters are installed on a wooden bearing plate or a concrete bond course as seen here. The plate is fastened with bolts set into the adobe walls. All rafters or vigas should have at least a 5½ inch bearing on the continuous wood plate and be nailed to it. Vigas may project through the wall. Adobes are set above and between the vigas to build up a parapet above the roof.

View of split cedar fencing installed as a ceiling over vigas. They have been cut into short lengths and nailed securely to the vigas at an angle. Ceiling will need no finishing. Split saplings, split or round poles, bundles of twigs or saplings, or short lengths of rough planking were used as ceilings in old adobes and topped with layers of bark, straw, or chamisa and an 8 to 12 inch layer of earth to form a roof. You might use an 8 to 12 inch bed of coarse pumice rolled smooth for insulation and as a base for a built up roof.

A good roof is all important because a leak can melt an entire wall. Top the ceiling with building paper and layers of felt mopped with hot tar and topped with gravel. A three ply roof is the minimum. Make the canales wide so that the flashing will not constrict them and extend them far enough so that water running from the canales will not do splash damage to the vulnerable adobe walls. A pitch to the roof aids in draining off water. Canales on the north are likely to be choked by ice in severe weather.

Brick floor being laid in sand. Blow sand (very fine sand which has been wind carried and dropped on the lee side of hills) is excellent for this. Note the use of the rubber hammer to set bricks firmly. Bricks may be laid in many patterns. The herringbone is laid along a diagonal string line and bricks are cut at an angle when the wall is reached. I once saw a beautiful carmel colored floor of large Roman bricks, special ordered without holes in the face, laid in a herringbone pattern which gave the effect of antique parquet flooring. It had been finished with sealer and required only occasional waxing.

Bricks may be sealed, waxed, or varnished. Sealing is perhaps most satisfactory. They can be "aged" by sanding with a heavy duty sanding machine and swabbing with used motor oil to darken them. Walls may be plastered down to the brick floor or a row of bricks set on edge around the walls as a base before plastering is done.

Experimental patch of mud plaster which proved to be unsatisfactory. Sand may be added to the dirt to prevent cracking. Blow sand is excellent. Soil had too much clay. Note large cracks and patch which failed to adhere. The plaster here was applied with a hand trowel. (Zonolite may be hand troweled for an acceptable mud plaster appearance.)

Cement can be added to the dry dirt for mud plaster to serve as a stabilizer. Use one or two shovelsful per wheelbarrow load. A test patch should be made to determine the right amount. This must be mixed in small batches as it sets up rather rapidly. Mix about what can be troweled on in 20 minutes and apply with a hand trowel. Dry wall texture can be painted on stabilized bricks or stabilized mud plaster. Plain adobe walls, dampened and brushed down to knock off loose particles, can also be finished with dry wall texture.

Pictures on pp. 197, 198, 203, and 204, bottom: photographer, Wm. R. Dickson.

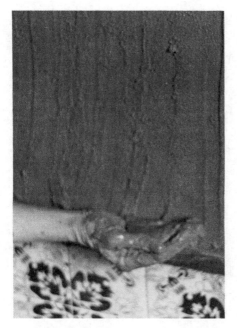

Mud plaster may also be applied by hand. The slip or scratch coat of mud plaster for hand application is much thinner than the final coat. It will spread when placed on a flat surface and will not retain indentations when fingers are inserted into it. Screen soil through coarse fly screen. Adequate mixing is essential. All of the mix must be equally moistened.

The scratch coat is applied with the cupped palm of the hand and spread upward with smooth straight strokes. Very little finger pressure is applied. Spreading is done with the flat of the hand. The scratch coat is not rubbed entirely smooth. When it is dry, dampen with a fine spray before adding finish coat.

Mud for the finish coat is a stiffer mix and will adhere to the wall when thrown on it by the handful.

Mud for the finish coat still slumps but will retain finger prints. Let mixed mud "rest" for a few minutes before applying it to the wall.

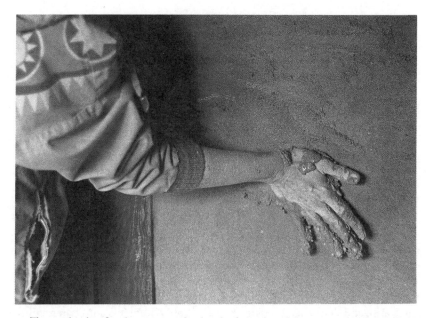

To apply the final coat use the heel of the hand keeping the fingers up. Throw on a handful and work the mud out fanwise to an even thickness. Don't try to smooth out all the little bumps and irregularities at first. Don't rub hard on any one area. After the coat has been applied let it dry briefly. Test a spot. When you rub it with the heel of your hand it should feel sandy and shouldn't look shiny. Begin to rub the wall using the flat of your hand in a hard round and round motion. Fingertips are used now. As you rub, fine "crumbs" will be rubbed off. When the entire surface has been rubbed allow the wall to dry still further. Use a fine brush, making short *light* dabs at the wall to knock the sand off. Stop if you notice a shiny spot. If this step is done right, no sand will shift from the wall later. Hands are those of Mrs. Howard DeVaney who was kind enough to pass along the details of the technique.

HOUSE PLANS

House Plan #1

La Hacienda Redondo is a modern adobe with clean contemporary lines. 18,000 baked adobe bricks from Mexico, treated with silicone for weather resistance, were used in its construction. They were laid with trinity white cement dyed to match the adobe color. Roof overhang and wooden grilles on the windows control the sun and add interest to the facade. Large groups may be easily entertained. Traffic flows through the family room, formal living room, and den with the entry hall as a hub. Kitchen is convenient with a pass-through into the family room and a door opening onto the patio. Den is fitted with a bar. Kitchen has ample counter and cupboard space, and a pantry in the center unit containing the fireplace provides bulk storage. Master suite features a divided bath with a sauna and well designed closet space. Designed and built by H. L. Cleff, Jr. with Joe Priestley.

House Plan #2

The formal living room was added after the house was completed. Location of the entry drive naturally funnels traffic to the portal entrance. Open plan allows circulation of large groups for entertaining. Plan could be built minus formal living room and dining room to accommodate a smaller family. Family kitchen has eating counter. The fireplace end of the room could be used for dining or as a sitting room as the C. A. Andersons have furnished it. The house is constructed of stabilized adobes requiring no exterior finish. Interior walls are painted with latex paint. The entry and family living room have brick floors; bedroom wing is carpeted.

House Plan #3

Home of Mr. and Mrs. N. J. Shetler in Corrales. House is spread out to capitalize on panoramic view from the site. All major rooms have an outside exit. Kitchen is centrally located. Double course walls were laid for the living room and master bedroom. A double thick wall may be laid with two 10-inch adobes laid 4 inches apart. Above 6 feet the outer wall may be brought in gradually until the two walls meet and meld. Change of wall height of the living room wing and the batter (inward slope) of the exterior walls add visual interest.

House Plan #4

Plumbing is concentrated, shape of house and exterior details were kept simple, salvaged materials were used, and owner did contracting to keep costs down. Exterior walls are 24 inches thick at front of house. Walls under portal are stabilized adobe. Outside walls except under portal are plastered. Inside walls were scrubbed down with sheep skin pads and painted. Floors are bricks laid in sand which were laid before house walls went up. Bricks were sanded with a heavy duty floor sander, "aged" by swabbing with used motor oil, and sealed. Ceilings are willow saplings with the bark left on woven into panels. Old redwood timbers and windows were salvaged from an old Santa Fe round house in El Paso. Old doors were used except for custom-made entry door, double doors in foyer, and hollow core doors covered with wall fabric. Kitchen accommodates a 60″ commercial range and has laminated wood counters. deWerd home, Corrales.

House Plan #5

Compact one bedroom plan. Attached carport to the rear and portal across the front give protection from the sun and increase the apparent size of the house. Living room is out of the traffic pattern yet hall space is minimal. A wooden grille from counter to ceiling would hide kitchen if an open kitchen is not desired. Floors are bricks laid in sand. Ceilings are decking on peeled vigas. Walls are plaster inside and out. Blue and white Mexican tile has been used at the base of the walls and as trim for a corner fireplace with great effect.

House Plan #6

The grouping of three fireplaces is a notable feature of this plan for an adobe home designed and constructed by the W. A. Bigneys. Kitchen has a fireplace, cozy sitting corner. Master bedroom is isolated from the family activity area and has access to the rear patio. Living room has a wall of bookshelves. Washer and dryer are located in bedroom wing, a step-saving arrangement. Exterior is traditional with territorial trim. Walls are plastered inside and out. Floors are bricks laid in sand. Future family room is plastered in mud plaster to which cement has been added.

House Plan #7

House designed and built by Happ Crawford has a free standing fireplace and a tiny balcony over one end of the living room reached by a circular iron stairway, illustrated elsewhere in the book. Dining and living area are separated by a change of level and a low partition. Kitchen has an island work center containing stove. Divided bath serves two bedrooms and as a "powder" room. Gallery seems spacious because it is opened to the patio by a row of windows. Floors are brick. Walls are plastered inside and out. Ceilings are stained wood. The high walls of the living room wing require buttresses. As a rule of thumb wall heights should not be more than ten times the wall thickness unless they can be stiffened by buttresses or intersecting partitions. One buttress has been made an architectural feature of the patio. Huge cottonwood tree roofs this area and controls the wind. A completely enclosed patio is not always successful because wind rolling over the house creates turbulence. Drainage of rainwater must also be provided for.

House Plan #8

Plan by Robert C. Koeber and Co., specialists in adobe construction, illustrates how a basic arrangement can be adapted and the exterior appearance changed by a rearrangement of components. The Jason Rogers home which was built by Mr. Koeber is a good example of a traditional exterior with a territorial trim which would be suitable for this plan.

House Plan #9

Small rectangular house with 1200 square feet of floor space. Any simple plan of this type should be suitable for adobe construction if a few rules are observed by the amateur builder-designer. The total width of openings in a wall should not exceed 40% of its length. Windows and doors should be located at least three feet from the corners, and wall sections between door and window openings should be at least 3 feet in length. Ceiling heights should be no more than nine feet.

House Plans #10 and #11

Two bedroom plans which present a long facade, extended by carports, to look larger than they are. Plan #10 is an excellent plan for a traditional treatment. It features a large entry hall opening onto the portal reminiscent of the *sala*. Closets on either side of the living room doorway create a deep archway. With two bathrooms and three fireplaces, this is not a minimum plan. R. C. Koeber & Co. Plan #11 separates the bedrooms for privacy. T-shaped plan allows each bedroom to have its own garden entrance. Plumbing is grouped for economy. Kitchen is centrally located. Living room does not get through traffic.

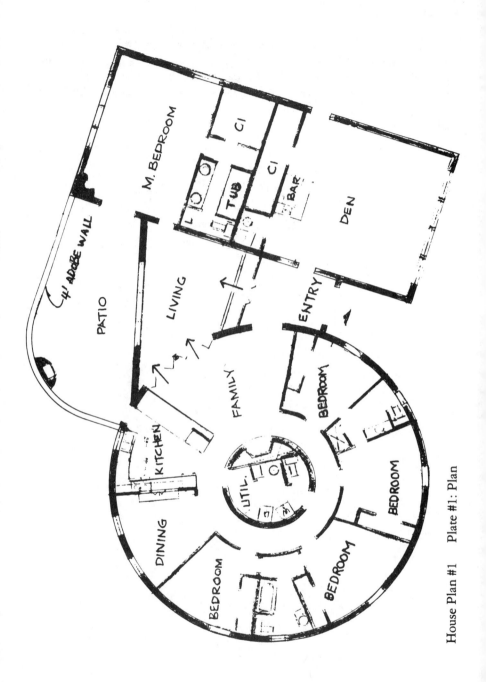

House Plan #1   Plate #1: Plan

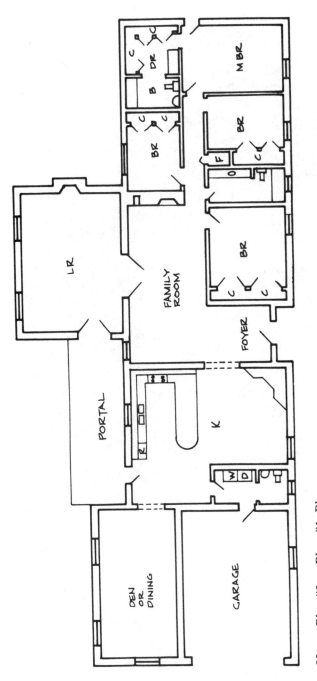

House Plan #2   Plate #1: Plan

Plate #2: Elevation

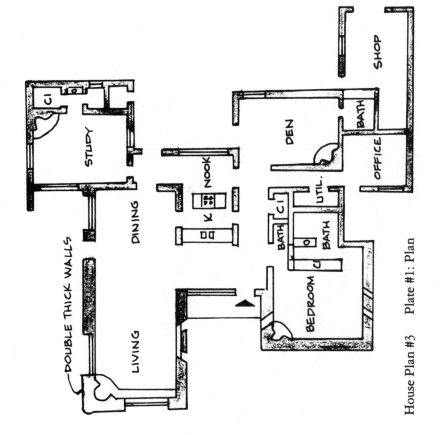

House Plan #3   Plate #1: Plan

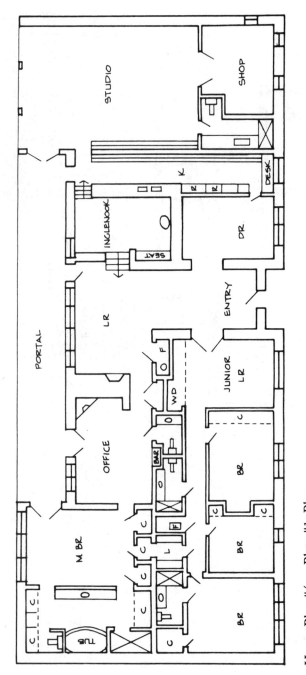

House Plan #4   Plate #1: Plan

Plate #2: Exterior

Plate #3: Portal. Stabilized adobes in wall were mixed in a pit large enough to accommodate a small tractor. The bituminous mix was poured in on the adobe mud. Amounts could only be approximate. The mud was mixed with a tractor with a front loader which was also used to fill the forms for the bricks. Forms were removed in two days and adobes were cured enough to use in two weeks.

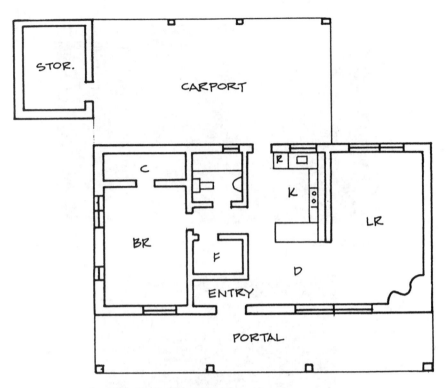

House Plan #5   Plate #1: Floor plan

Plate #2: Wall at left encloses a small patio. Portal shades the large windows which open the house to a view of the nearby mountains.

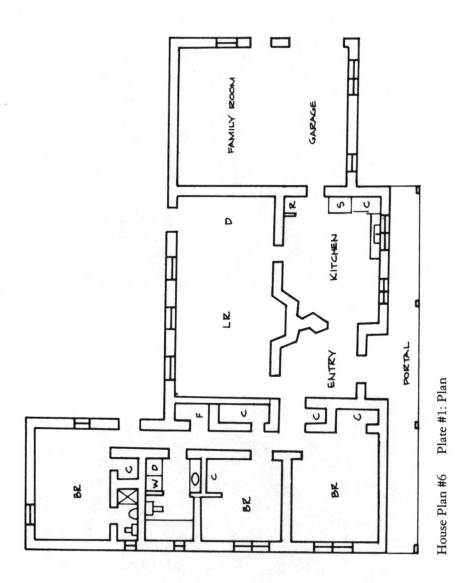

House Plan #6   Plate #1: Plan

Plate #3: Barbecue is architectural feature of the patio. Door to gallery is at right.

Plate #2: Open patio door can be seen under the portal. Living room wing on the right.

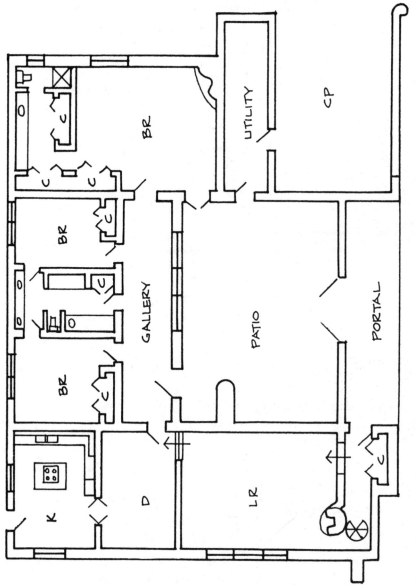

House Plan #7   Plate #1: Floor plan

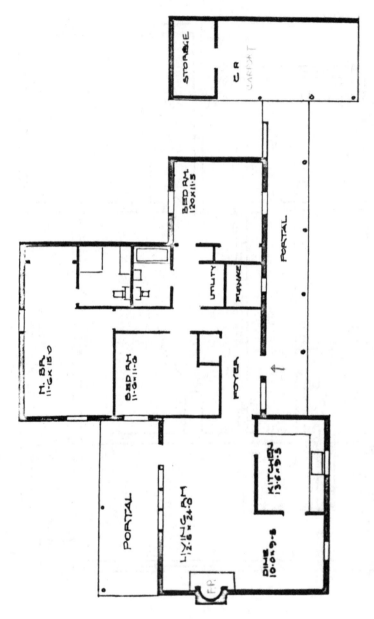

House Plan #8   Plate #1: Plan

Plate #2: Jason Rogers home.

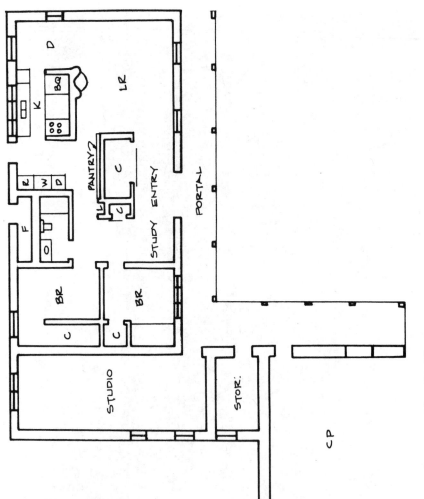

House Plan #9   Plate #1: Plan

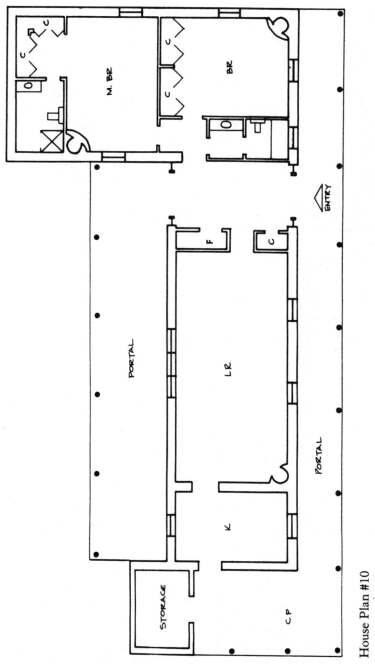

House Plan #10

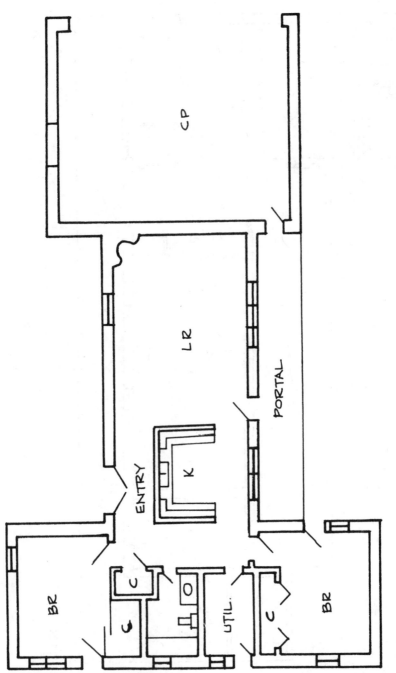

House Plan #11

INDEX